# "AFTER ALL WE'VE DONE FOR THEM"

# "AFTER ALL, WE'VE DONE FOR THEM"

## Understanding Adolescent Behavior

## Louis L. Fine, M.D.

PRENTICE-HALL, INC., Englewood Cliffs, New Jersey

*"After All We've Done for Them": Understanding Adolescent Behavior,*
by Louis L. Fine, M.D.

Printed in the United States of America

Prentice-Hall International, Inc., London
Prentice-Hall of Australia, Pty. Ltd., Sydney
Prentice-Hall of Canada, Ltd., Toronto
Prentice-Hall of India Private Ltd., New Delhi
Prentice-Hall of Japan, Inc., Tokyo
Prentice-Hall of Southeast Asia Pte. Ltd., Singapore
Whitehall Books Limited, Wellington, New Zealand

10 9 8 7 6 5 4 3 2 1

Library of Congress Cataloging in Publication Data

Fine, Louis L
  After all we've done for them: understanding
adolescent behavior.
  Includes index.
  1. Adolescence.    2. Adolescent psychology.
3. Parent and child.    4. Conflict of generations.
I. Title.
HQ796.F57        301.43'15        77-22390
ISBN 0-13-018432-2

To my family, who parented me,
and to my daughter, Lisa,
whom I have the pleasure of parenting

# Contents

# Introduction

"After all we've done for them . . ." has been the lament of parents for centuries as they reflect upon the often contrary and contradictory behavior of their adolescent children. At no time in life do the struggles between parent and offspring emerge so intensely as during adolescence. The turmoil often causes parents to forget that adolescence is a developmental bridge between childhood and adulthood and that it is not a terminal stage of one's personal growth.

The process of adolescence is perhaps as difficult for parents as for adolescents themselves. While the adolescent forges (or fumbles) ahead, searching for answers to life's questions through behavioral experimentation, parents are left to worry about dangerous consequences of the behavior—the consequences of which the adolescent often seems completely unaware.

The behavior of an adolescent frequently evokes feelings of anger, hostility, frustration, and resentment in his parents. The behavior of parents frequently evokes feelings of anger, hostility, frustration, and resentment in the adolescent. The inevitable clash can be destructive to both—but need not be to either.

The purpose of this book is to enable both parents and adolescents to gain insights into why they feel and behave as they do when confronted with the emotionally-charged issues of adolescence—drugs, sex, parental conflicts, school, friends, illness, physical appearance, and the generation gap. Understanding why we think and act the way we do can diminish tensions and anxieties, change conflict into growth, and allow us to function more effectively—as a parent or as an adolescent.

Parents who love their children may help them grow and be happy or may stunt their growth and cause them unhappiness. Love, by itself, is not enough. For example, loving a plant does not ensure that we will care for it properly: We may give the plant too much water and kill it; we may give it too little water and kill it. As long as we water according to *our* preconceived ideas about the plant's needs, we may do it harm. When we appreciate and understand the needs of the *plant* and water it accordingly, our nurturing will help it to thrive.

A similar situation exists with our children. We love our children; however, if we treat them according to *our perception* of their needs rather than to *their actual* needs, we risk impairing their growth and happiness.

And that is what this book is all about—recognizing and appreciating the needs of our teenage children so that we can help them to grow, to prosper, and to be happy.

Louis L. Fine, M.D.

**On the use of "he" and "she" in this book:** In writing this book, it was difficult to avoid using "he" or "she" and "him" or "her" in situations applying to both sexes. Our language doesn't have a singular pronoun that means *either* a boy or a girl. I don't like "s/he" and find alternating "she" and "he" awkward. ("It" hardly seems appropriate.) When the material applies primarily to girls, I have used "she," and when it applies primarily to boys, I have used "he." For the most part, however, "he" refers to a teenager of either sex.

L.L.F.

# "AFTER ALL WE'VE DONE FOR THEM"

# 1

# "When I Was Their Age..."

The familiar lament beginning "When I was their age..." has been echoed by the parents of adolescents for countless generations. Even Socrates, 2,500 years ago, had some difficulty understanding adolescent behavior. He observed: "They now seem to love luxury, they have bad manners and contempt for authority, they show disrespect for adults and spend their time hanging around places gossiping with one another. They are ready to contradict their parents, monopolize the conversation and company, eat gluttonously and tyrannize their teachers." ...

Adolescence is not new—it has always existed as a developmental bridge between childhood and adulthood. Yet, however contemporary Socrates' statement may appear, there are marked differences between the youth of yesteryear and those of today. Two essential differences are that the freedom to indulge in the behavioral process of adolescence is available to more youth, and that adolescence is more prolonged than ever before. In the past, most youngsters were supposed to be like their parents when they grew up, and only a few fortunate teenagers had the freedom and opportunity to explore lifestyles and identities markedly different from those of their parents. Now, more youth have the opportunity to develop an identity which is based upon their own self-actualization rather than upon the expectations of of their parents and society. The longer duration of adolescence as a period of freedom from adult responsibilities is also relatively recent. Even in the late nineteenth century, children did not have to attend school, and many went to work at quite an early age. There was precious little time for most adolescents to "do their own thing" or just "hang out." Society was relatively stable, and children undertook adultlike responsibilities out of economic necessity. In the early 1900s, two pieces of social legislation were enacted which opened the door of adolescence for the majority of teenagers. One was the passage of child labor laws which stated that children could no longer be used in the economic production scheme. The second was the passage of compulsory education laws, which required children to attend school. The effect of these laws was to free youth from the necessity of taking on adultlike responsibilities, and therefore youngsters had more time to behave as adolescents.

Increasingly in the twentieth century, America has evolved from an industrial society into a technological one. Never before has there been a society with as high a level of technological development and material affluence. Such a society requires high levels of education of its citizens, and no previous society has ever had so many being educated for so long. Today, approximately half of our high school graduates continue on to college, and half of our college graduates go on to pursue postgraduate education.

The material resources of our country give teenagers that luxury of affluence—free time. We simply do not require our youth to be economically productive; we do require them to become highly educated. Thus our youth are in a relatively unique situation—a situation in which they have years of freedom from adult responsibilities during which they can experiment and "do their own thing" as well as complete their educations. Never before have so many of our youth led such safe, secure, and affluent lives, and had the opportunity to "act like adolescents." Most teenagers make use of this free time by undergoing the once-rare self-actualization process called adolescence.

Many of us have heard someone say (or wanted to say ourselves) to an idle teenager: "You lazy bum! Why don't you get a job?" The truth is, we should probably be glad he's *not* working—if he were, an adult might not be. There are approximately 40 million adolescents today; our economy simply cannot accommodate such numbers of relatively unskilled workers.

Many adults perceive the "idle" adolescent behavior of today as quite different from their own working adolescent behavior. Many question: "Where did we go wrong? Has society failed?" Society has not failed. On the contrary, it has succeeded beyond expectation—succeeded enough to create an environment where most adolescents simply don't have to work on a full-time basis. The work ethic that has traditionally buttressed our society no longer appears highly relevant to many adolescents as they view their own affluent and secure lives. The adult ethic is oriented toward the future, achievement, work, and delay of gratification, while teenagers have a much more *present-oriented, becoming-oriented,* and *idealistic* ethic. Although there are many and varied reasons for these differences, one is of particular importance: *Society no longer gives an identity to the individual; it is up to the individual to seek out his own identity.* While searching for and defining one's own adult identity, one engages in present-oriented and becoming-oriented (Who am I?) behavioral experimentation. Until one's identity begins to form, it is very difficult to delay gratification and plan for the future.

Parents who say "When I was their age, things were different" are right—things *were* different. Society and its values have changed, and today's teenagers live in quite a different environment from that in which their parents grew up. The new freedom and mobility of this environment have also brought difficulties. Rapid social change has caused a relative lack of consensus and conviction regarding many of society's values. The decline of the nuclear family, changing moral values, and the widespread feeling that people should "do their own thing" affect both parents and adolescents. Parents are deprived of widespread family and community support in their child-rearing practices; adolescents are deprived of the benefit of relatively clear-cut limits and guidelines for their behavior. The decline of firmly held values and beliefs among parents and throughout society makes it more difficult for the adolescent to establish his own value system as he develops a self-identity. Perhaps this is the special adaptation required of today's youth—to learn how to live with constant change, uncertainty, and ambiguity of values.

Another problem for the adolescent is the absence of well-defined behavioral models with whom he can identify and pattern his behavior in bridging the gap between childhood and adulthood. Often the early adolescent looks toward the older adolescent as a behavioral model, but here he often finds much confusion because the most publicized groups of adolescents appear to be those who are most in conflict with society (and with themselves).

I have spoken of the necessity for an adolescent to develop and establish his or her own identity. But identity is not static—it's a dynamic, fluctuating conception of self that varies with one's age and changes in society's values. In order to understand an adolescent's behavior, we must consider how he functions within his environment. We cannot analyze a teenager's behavior apart from his environment. Therefore, an awareness of how society influences adolescents is crucial, for it provides us with a frame of reference in which to judge the appropriateness or inappropriateness of their behavior—behavior that affects all of us.

# 2

# "After All We've Done for Them..."

One of the problems facing adolescents is that, whether they show it or not, they *do* realize all you've done for them. They know that you have cared for and nurtured them, have made sacrifices on their behalf, and have tried to be good parents. So why are they acting this way? What's happening to them? Must there be conflict between parents and their adolescents? To answer these questions we must ask another question: What is a normal adolescent?...

An adolescent's behavior is frequently bewildering to his family, his friends, and even to himself. This chapter will describe the ever-changing and complex behavior pattern typical of adolescents and explain the necessity of such behavior. By understanding why your adolescent behaves as he or she does, you can diminish much of the usual pain, confusion, and frustration that may be caused by adolescent behavior. An adolescent is neither a child nor an adult; his behavior, therefore, should not be judged by either childhood or adult standards. Adolescent behavior should be evaluated in terms of the purposes and processes of that unique period of growth called adolescence.

## THE PURPOSES OF ADOLESCENCE

### The Psychologic Developmental Tasks

Adolescence represents a developmental bridge between childhood and adulthood. An adolescent must successfully complete certain psychologic developmental tasks in order to become an emotionally mature and normal adult. An understanding of these tasks can help provide organization, logic, and meaning to an otherwise bewildering, confusing, and often seemingly purposeless array of adolescent behavior. There are four basic adolescent psychologic developmental tasks, emotional milestones that the adolescent must reach to become an adult.

The first task for the adolescent is to develop and establish a stable, realistic, positive, adult *self-identity*. In the past, society assigned to each individual an identity based on birthright, wealth, or ethnic group. Today, society no longer provides such a defined social identity, and the adolescent must discover and define his own self-identity.

The second task of adolescence is to become *emancipated from parents* and other adults, and this task is most difficult.

Torn between the wish to be taken care of as a child and the increasing urge to take care of himself, the adolescent undergoes what might be called an "independent-dependent struggle" both within himself and with his parents.

The third task is to acquire the skills necessary for future economic independence. This has to do with one's career plans and represents the *vocational orientation* of the adolescent.

The fourth task is psychosexual differentiation—that is, learning to function as a man or as a woman in an *adult heterosexual role*.

## THE PROCESSES OF ADOLESCENCE

A technique often used by adolescents as they attempt to accomplish the developmental tasks is behavioral experimentation. To be able to afford the luxury of behavioral experimentation, adolescents need both time and resources. Modern child labor and compulsory education laws provide the necessary time, and our affluent society provides the necessary resources. Freedom from early assumption of adult responsibilities allows adolescents to experiment with differing patterns of behavior. Such experimentation accounts for much of the paradoxical and complex activities that are characteristic of adolescence.

Other processes of adolescence include the apparent rejection of many parental values, alienation from parents themselves, and the independent-dependent struggle adolescents undergo with their parents and other adults.

## THE STAGES OF ADOLESCENT BEHAVIOR

To determine whether an adolescent's behavior is normal or indicative of problems, and to determine what progress has been made in accomplishing the developmental tasks, it is helpful to view adolescence as divided into three psychologically distinct stages: early, middle, and late adolescence. A youngster begins early adolescence by first casting off his childlike role and image. This stage of emotional development is very difficult, and is perhaps the unhappiest stage. Middle adolescence is marked by peer group activities and intense involvement in the adolescent subculture; at this stage friends become very important. Late adolescence is characterized by the emergence of adult behavior.

In all three stages of psychological development, the adolescent functions in three different social areas: at *home*, within the *peer group*, and at *school*. Therefore, you should assess how your adolescent is functioning in each of these three areas and whether his behavior in *all* of these areas is normal for his stage of development.

One's chronological age (years old) may be quite different from one's psychologic or emotional age (mental maturity). Since individuals mature psychologically at various chronologic ages, it is important to assess their behavior in terms of psychological development as well as chronologic age.

## Early Adolescence

Entrance into adolescence is marked by behavior that begins to sever previous *dependent emotional ties* the adolescent has had with his parents. The early adolescent may become less involved in family activities, tend to downgrade his parents, and become increasingly reluctant to accept adult advice or criticism. Frequently the hobbies that tied him to a childhood image or role are discarded, and no longer is he compliant, agreeable, and disciplined. Such behavioral patterns are hallmarks of the beginning independent-dependent struggle. The emerging adolescent retains many *dependent* needs for love, food, shelter, clothing, and emotional support, yet in many ways he desires *independence* from his parents. It is as if the adolescent convinces himself that he no longer needs his parents—for if he needed, and was dependent upon, his parents in *all* ways, how could he ever begin to separate from them and to stand on his own two feet? Such emotional separation between adolescent and parents, though painful to both, makes it easier for the teenager to enter into adolescent behavior and begin to accomplish the developmental tasks. If everything were perfect between adolescent and parent, it would be difficult to change preexisting relationships and roles; a little friction in the relationship makes separation easier. For example, Johnny began to find fault with his mother's cooking and housecleaning, and with his father's being away from home too much. Johnny's fault-finding made his parents seem less "perfect," and his critical attitude created friction between him and his parents. These disagreements facilitated Johnny's emotional separation from his parents. Much of the ambivalent behavior an adolescent exhibits toward his parents (one minute a caring darling; the next, a snotty brat) stems from his struggles to attain emotional separation.

The behavior of a normal early adolescent frequently causes his parents to become quite angry. His change from a dependent, childlike role to a more independent status makes him harder for his parents to control. He is no longer the obedient child, but a questioning, talking-back, testing-out adolescent. When worried parents describe such behavior, I feel like saying, "Welcome to the club! Your child is now an adolescent."

Parents should understand that some provoking, alienating behavior is normal, even necessary, and should be expected from the early and middle adolescent. Such behavior helps him to dissipate and defend against the pain and guilt that he frequently feels as he relinquishes his previous childhood roles. Awareness of this may diminish significantly the tensions and anxieties that often exist between parent and teenager and may even enable parents to help smooth their children's transition into adolescence. For example, Robert, aged fourteen, began to talk back to his parents and act "smart-alecky." This behavior was very irritating, but his parents understood that it was typical of an early adolescent. Instead of becoming angry at Robert and punishing him, they told him that they realized he was growing up and were willing to give him more freedom and responsibility. His parents' understanding of the meaning of the irritating behavior enabled them to respond in a way that decreased the necessity for Robert to continue it, eased tensions in the family, and smoothed his entry into adolescence.

School provides a nonparental structured environment in which the adolescent can learn more about authority and authority limits. It is also a place to plan for future vocational goals. Poor school attendance and falling grades are sensitive indicators, and are often the first clue, that an adolescent is having emotional or adjustment problems. Although many adolescents complain about school, what really counts is their *performance*. I've often had the following conversation with an early or middle adolescent:

> *"How's school?"*
> "I hate it!"
> *"How're your teachers?"*
> "Terrible!"
> *"What kind of school grades did you get last semester?"*
> "Well ... I made the honor role."
> *"How many days of school have you missed this year?"*
> "None."
> *"How's school?"*
> "I hate it!"

*Or:*

"*How's school?*"
"I love it!"
"*How're your teachers?*"
"Great!"
"*What kind of school grades did you get last semester?*"
"Well . . . not too good. I failed two courses."
"*How many days of school have you missed this year?*"
"Well, I've been cutting a lot and . . ."
"*How's school?*"
"I love it!"

Actions do speak louder than words. Reports from school teachers can provide helpful information about your adolescent's social as well as scholarly performance.

***Summary of early adolescence*** Emotional conflicts that occur during early adolescence center on the adolescent's loss of his previous childhood identity. Until he becomes involved in the peer group and adolescent subculture that mark middle adolescence, a psychological void may exist; he is neither completely dependent upon his parents nor fully accepted into the peer group. Conflicts may lead to mood swings accompanied by depression and boredom, temporary retreats back into childlike behavior, self-centered and *mildly* antisocial behavior, *slight* fall in school grades, and *occasional* truancy.

Thirteen-year-old Sharon began spending most of her free time in her room, listening to records. Her school grades dropped from A's to B's. Her parents found it nearly impossible to discuss anything with her, because at the slightest disagreement she would begin either shouting or crying. Nothing her family did seemed to please her, and she complained that her parents were "dumb" and didn't "understand" her.

An adult who exhibited comparable behavior patterns would probably be considered to have serious emotional problems; in early adolescence, however, such behavior is usually normal. This emphasizes why one should not judge the normality or abnormality of an adolescent's behavior by adult standards but according to the purposes and processes of his stage of development. The purposes of the early adolescent stage can be summarized as the casting off of childhood and the emergence into adolescence. The main processes are the questioning and rejection of many parental values, the beginning of the independent-dependent struggle, and "testing-out" behavioral experimentation.

If a teenager exhibits no rejection whatsoever of family or teachers, this probably means that he or she has not yet entered adolescence and that emotional problems may exist. An early adolescent who repeatedly refuses to go to school or who never spends time with friends is exhibiting an abnormal adjustment. School failure, school dropout, and frequent or solo drug use are other indications of possible emotional problems.

## Middle Adolescence

Middle adolescence is marked by strong peer group allegiances and involvement in the "adolescent subculture." Through development of emotional ties with the peer group, the middle adolescent attempts to fill the psychologic void left by the casting-off of close childhood dependence upon parents. As peer group loyalties develop, *friends* become very important, seemingly more important than parents. The middle adolescent may adopt many of the peer group's ideas and values and assume the role of the modern teenager by actively participating in contemporary fads of dress, language, music, and dance. It's almost as if the adolescent is thinking: "If I really don't look like my parents, don't dress like them, don't talk like them, and have different ideas, music, and dance—then maybe I really am *different* [separate] from them." The peer group provides the self-conscious, emotionally unsure and anxious adolescent with needed psychologic support in his attempts to achieve emotional separation from his parents and to establish a "separate" identity. The identity achieved by the middle adolescent is *separate only in reference to parents and other adults; it is very conforming in regard to peers.* For example, Mr. and Mrs. W are always well groomed, conservatively dressed, and well mannered. They consider their fifteen-year-old son, Dustin, nothing less than a disaster area. He is unkempt, dresses faddishly, and has a marked distaste for social niceties. His hair and clothes are so similar to those of his friends that sometimes Dustin's parents have to look twice to see which one is their son. They know that he smokes; they suspect that he drinks; they are worried about what else he might be doing with those friends of his. Dustin is definitely in middle adolescence. On the other hand, I recently saw a fifteen-year-old boy come into a restaurant with his parents. He looked like a miniature version of his father, had a crew cut, wore a three-piece dark suit with a necktie, and pulled out the chair for his mother. I would guess that he has not yet entered adolescence.

Although peer group dynamics and relationships do not foster individual functioning and identity, what the middle adolescent seeks in the peer group is not a *distinct* identity but a *stable* identity. He needs the *group identity* of an adolescent, not necessarily that of a separate, distinct individual. The creation of differences by the peer group (the generation gap) helps the adolescent by reinforcing his own feelings of being different from his parents and thus facilitates emotional separation. (The need to be separate must be great —why else would so many go to such extremes to be "different"?)

The nonadult arena of the peer group is also crucial to

psychological development, for it is within this parentless group that one can conduct behavioral experimentation and progress through the developmental tasks. Friends (the nonadult peer group) condone and even encourage behavioral experimentation in peer-accepted behavioral patterns. The adolescent's peer group relationships and activities can provide valuable information regarding his progress through the developmental tasks. If he has significant difficulties with his peer group, he may have adjustment problems.

However, all is not rosy with the adolescent and his peer group. Since the interpersonal relationships within the peer group are often superficial and one's individuality is highly compromised to group values, emotional conflicts frequently occur. The loss of one's individuality to the group is a primary reason for the eventual demise of the peer group. As one's own self-identity becomes established, one is able to make one's own decisions and to rely less and less on peer group values.

Expected "normal" middle adolescent activities may include *occasional* group antisocial behavior or even a *partial* hippie-type dropout. Risk-taking may occur as the middle adolescent tries to prove himself to be fearless, powerful, or sexy. Abnormal or pathologic adjustments exist when an adolescent is friendless, has poor peer group ties, or is sexually promiscuous. Frequent or solo drug use almost always indicates significant adjustment problems.

The peer group is so important to the psychological development of the adolescent that it is fair to say *an adolescent without friends is an adolescent in trouble* and in need of professional help.

## Late Adolescence

Late adolescence is characterized by further emotional emancipation and the assumption of adult roles. Severing *physical* ties with the family may require one to move into one's own apartment or residence. The late adolescent becomes more nearly self-sufficient financially and begins to accept additional adult responsibilities and roles. The principal growth task is to become a competent, worthwhile, independent adult.

"Normal" adjustment problems occur when the late adolescent feels hesitant in accepting independent responsibility and maintains middle adolescent roles by continued emotional dependence on the peer group. An abnormal situation exists when middle adolescent roles persist and, on occasion, late adolescence simply never occurs.

For example, after Roy graduated from high school he couldn't decide whether he wanted to go to college, attend trade school, or get a job, so he decided to stay at home. He liked his room and enjoyed his mother's cooking. He continued to go out with the remaining members of his high school group. Despite frequent arguments with his parents, Roy remains at home and has no plans for his future.

*Summary of stages* /The adolescent is less concerned with his behavior than he is with the questions he is attempting to answer through his behavior. Behavioral experimentation, some rejection of parents and parental values, "normal" alienation from parents, and the independent-dependent struggle are all processes utilized in the adolescent's endeavor to accomplish the developmental tasks. The concepts of psychologic developmental tasks and stages of adolescence provide a useful framework by which to understand an adolescent's behavior.

## REFLECTION

"After all we've done for him, how can he talk to us that way?"

I frequently hear such a lament from distraught parents.

If the adolescent is doing well at school, has appropriate peer group activities, and is really *not* a discipline problem at home, I often say to the parents: "Good! You've done your job. Why do you raise your children? To be able to stand on their own feet. To be adults. Well, it looks like that's starting. It must be nice to have a son [or daughter] who can say what he wants. You might not like what he says, but he *is* standing on his own two feet. No wishy-washy child did you raise, but one with his own ideas and convictions. In fact, as parents, you've really succeeded."

# 3

# Parents Are Parents . . . Friends Are Friends

He was wearing a beret, a flowered shirt open at the neck, bell-bottomed fade-out jeans, a well-trimmed moustache and a goatee, and as he greeted me he flashed a peace sign. This is not a caricature—he was a real-life person. Another adolescent patient? No, this was the father of one. Of course, we cannot judge a person by his appearance, but this man may be one of those parents who need introduction to the concept of: Parents are parents . . . friends are friends. . . .

All too frequently, parents of adolescents become confused about their proper parental roles. There are significant differences between being friendly with your adolescent and being his friend. Your adolescent doesn't want you as a friend, your adolescent wants you as a parent—a friendly parent, but a parent nevertheless. An adolescent needs and requires different things from his parents than he does from his friends. Parents should serve as real-life models for adult behavior and must care enough to tell their children what to do—to be the limit-setters, the disciplinarians. *Parents must be parents.* On the other hand, friends (the nonparent peer group) are needed to accept and even encourage various behavioral experiments which parents cannot condone but which may be necessary for completion of the adolescent's developmental tasks. Within the peer group, an adolescent's testing-out and experimentation may result in his being considered "groovy," and thereby enhance his peer acceptance.

Parents may also try to act "groovy," perhaps to gain their adolescent's acceptance or to achieve increased communication with him. In many parents, however, attempts at "grooviness" reflect their desire to be adolescents themselves. Most parents of adolescents are in their late thirties to mid-forties, a stage of adult life that is being increasingly recognized as a time of emotional upheaval and stress. Frequently, adults at this stage of life begin to question seriously and to reappraise their own life-styles, roles, and values. Many have attained the "success" for which they have so diligently strived, but now that these goals are reached, they may be found to be less enjoyable and fulfilling than anticipated.

Many of today's parents of adolescents were themselves the adolescents of the fifties, a time when the prevailing ethic was highly future-oriented, achievement-oriented, and work-oriented. Many adults perceive the adolescent ethic of today as romantic, caring, and sharing, and many find it more appealing than the sarcastic one-upmanship that typified adolescent behavior of the fifties. It is no small wonder then that many adults, who are having their own adjustment problems, *fantasize* that today's present-oriented adolescents have found the answers they have not found themselves.

At the very time, therefore, when adolescents are undergoing emotional struggles, many of their parents are having similar difficulties. Marriage compromises that parents may have made (for example, "We'll stay married until the kids grow up") are losing their validity. Parents may begin to redefine their own future roles and responsibilities. Many divorces occur during this period of family upheaval.

Parents who act "groovy" (a once-fashionable in-group word, now dated, that can be translated as "in a manner characteristic of the youth culture") must recognize that their need to be groovy is quite different from the adolescent's need to be groovy. It's almost a truism: If the parents are groovy, their kids are straight (that is, adultlike); when the parents are straight, their kids are groovy. This paradox makes sense when we realize that adolescents want to be different from their parents, a need vividly reflected in the "generation gap." The so-called generation gap between adolescents and their parents is a healthy and important psychological phenomenon, the result of an adolescent's efforts to create an *emotional separation* between himself and his parents.

It is a very difficult and painful process for the early adolescent to begin emotional separation from his parents and to give up the security of a dependent child-parent relationship. The emotional upheaval inherent in the change from childhood to adolescence usually produces a great deal of stress for both adolescent and parent as previous patterns of parental control change. (It's easier to rule a child than to rule an adolescent).

Alienation is a process that serves to lessen the subconscious guilt most adolescents feel as they cast off their childhood roles and begin emotional separation from their parents. If you're "angry" at someone, if friction exists in the relationship, it becomes quite a bit easier to separate emotionally and, eventually, physically.

Such emotional separation helps the adolescent to accomplish two of the basic adolescent growth tasks: emancipation from parents and establishment of a separate self-identity. Perhaps if an adolescent looks, talks, and acts differently from his parents, he can more easily think of himself as separate from them. In being distinctly different from his parents, he does *not* want to have to be different from his friends. Therefore, *if the parents act groovy, this can be very confusing to the adolescent; he neither expects nor needs such behavior from his parents.*

In short: Parents are parents. Friends are friends.

The recent and rapid changes in our society seem to have magnified the difficulties between the adolescent and his parents. Geographic isolation from the extended family has increased the problems of many parents. In the past, parents could turn to close-by family members or friends for advice and assistance in their child-rearing practices and problems. In today's highly transient society, with relatives often far away, long-term friendships rare, and a wide range of cultural values within the community, parents frequently lack easy access to support for their own concepts of how to raise children. It is not only that parents are reinforced in their beliefs by living in a close-knit, homogeneous community, but also that adolescents are more likely to accept parental limits and standards when they see that these values are shared by other parents. Thus when *all* the adolescents have more or less the same rules and standards of dating, drugs, car use, school performance, being home by a certain hour, sexual mores, and behavioral expectations, it is less likely that the *individual* adolescent will question strenuously the limits set by his own parents. When parents from different families share similar values, they *reinforce* each other's beliefs, and the task of parenting adolescents is made that much easier. If, on the other hand, as is often the case today, parents do not communicate effectively with one another on child-rearing practices or if they disagree to a significant degree, the opportunities are ripe for such "adolescent blackmail" as: "But all the *other* kids can do it," "But *Johnny* doesn't have to be home till eleven," "But Joan is even younger than me and *she* can date," and so on. The adolescent himself can become deeply confused about the diversity of mores, values, beliefs, and standards he sees among his peer's parents.

This is all the more reason why parents have to act like parents. It is not always *easy*, but it is *mandatory*, for parents to set reasonable limits for their adolescents. Too often, laissez-faire means "I don't care." *If you as a parent care about the youngster for whom you are responsible, you must be prepared at times to tell him what to do.* You try to keep him from hurting himself. If you don't care about someone, what he does is usually of little concern to you. If you do care, let it be known, not only by statements of approval, but also by statements of disapproval. Parents and adolescents obviously cannot read each other's minds, and expectations must be expressed.

An adolescent's acting-out and defiant behavior may represent a general testing-out of adult rules and regulations; it may also specifically test out his parents: Will they care enough to tell him to stop or limit unacceptable behavior? What many adolescents really *need* and *want* from their parents is *limits placed on their behavior*—to have their parents act like parents. The adolescent's own family should be the first setting in which he can learn about behavioral expectations, limits, and responsibilities. It is within this framework, this family environment, that the foundation for self-control, self-discipline, and character structure is laid.

Although personality and character formation has been taking place for years, it is during the adolescent period that a teenager defines and strengthens his internal controls.

External controls are the environmental or social influences that dictate behavior, such as written and unwritten laws of society, limits placed by parents, peer group pressures, school rules and regulations, and the more general and often ambiguous mores of society. Life is not a free-form, free-association situation, but a structured environment of rules, regulations, and expectations. To live within a society, one has to abide largely by the rules—the external controls. The home is the initial environment for learning how to function within a framework of limits.

The internal controls are those decisions a person makes himself that determine his behavior. Although external controls always influence our decisions, every person, we hope, will also be able to make decisions based upon his own internal value system and do what is right, even if it clashes on occasion with the external controls.

It takes time to develop ego strengths, personality strengths, confidence in one's own abilities—all a part of internal controls. Throughout childhood, external controls exerted by parents, peers, and school dictate one's behavior. This is necessary to allow the gradual evolution of one's internal controls. If a child has had the security of home, parents, and parental limits, he has a better chance to develop and solidify his internal controls during adolescence. Adolescents begin to establish self-identity by testing the rules and beginning to utilize internal mechanisms in decision-making. If there are no rules, limits, or parental expectations to test-out against, the development of one's internal controls may be diffuse and disorganized. Many adolescents use testing-out behavior as a means of discovering and defining the rules, or the external controls, with which they must learn to live.

Such is frequently the case with an adolescent girl who acts-out sexually and then lets her parents discover her promiscuity. Although this may be done for several reasons, it is frequently an attempt to get parents to set limits (parental external controls) on behavior. I have often heard an acting-out adolescent ask: "Why didn't they [my parents] tell me to stop?" "Groovy" parents may respond: "Okay, it's your thing, and don't forget to take your birth control pills," but they are definitely *not* providing the behavioral guidelines or limits adolescents need and require. Most adolescents desperately *want* their parents to place restrictions on their behavior. Although adolescents may certainly gripe and complain, limits (external controls) provide them with a structure within which they can behave comfortably. Adolescents usually feel more emotionally secure when they have rules and guidelines to function by; they may become very anxious and insecure without external rules or structures for their behavior.

Frequently, therefore, two contrasting and conflicting social pressures are exerted on the developing adolescent: parental expectations of acceptable adultlike behavior, and peer group approval of adolescent behavioral experimentation. Parents are expected to tell an adolescent what to do; friends are expected to accept an adolescent's behavior. Parents should be friendly with their adolescent, but the relationship should be on a parent-adolescent basis and not on a peer-peer basis. It is not just okay, it's *mandatory*, for parents to set limits and tell their adolescents what to do!

Once again: Parents are parents . . . friends are friends.

# 5

# Obesity During Adolescence

One does not wake up fat. One has to work at it. One has to eat, and eat, and eat, and eat, and eat. It takes time, effort, and a willingness to eat, and eat, and eat. One doesn't magically find oneself fat. . . .

We all know people who are overweight, plump, heavy, or well fed. We may even describe them as such. But fat? No! Not her! She's just overweight, plump, heavy, or well fed. What a wonderful personality! What a cute face! Fat? No, not her! We also know people who are obese—they may be overweight, plump, heavy, or well fed; but they are also obese. Let's face it. If we like someone, we are quite reluctant to label him or her "fat"; yet if we don't particularly care for someone, we are quite willing to label him or her "fat." Fatness, or obesity, does tend to be regarded as a negative characteristic.

Obesity is not merely a tonnage problem. An obese person's weight influences life-style, social relationships, self-image, body concept, sexual identity, and personal activities. Since one doesn't suddenly find oneself obese, it is helpful to analyze some of the reasons that might drive someone to eat. By understanding the bases of obesity in adolescents, we can begin to develop insights into their problems, realize why diets usually fail, understand how well-intentioned parents can unwittingly contribute to their adolescent's overeating, and learn how parents can help their adolescents lose weight. We must consider the *total* human being and not be preoccupied with the surrounding fat.

## TYPES OF OBESITY

**Constitutional Obesity**/Although the vast majority of obese adolescents gained their weight from overeating, there are a few adolescents who are *constitutionally obese*. The constitutionally obese adolescent is one with a genetic, biochemical, or physiological tendency to become and remain overweight. This is usually the case where one or both parents are themselves obese, and these individuals are probably born with more and larger adipose (fat) cells. In this situation, one might be called "genetically obese." It is very difficult for these individuals to lose weight. They are usually emotionally well adjusted and take their large frame and body mass in stride. They are just big people. Many people who believe that they are constitutionally obese are not; they are overweight because of excessive caloric intake, often a result of their family's eating patterns.

**Developmental Obesity**/The developmentally obese adolescent is one who had a normal weight at birth but in the first years of life gained excessive weight, became obese, and has remained fat.

Infants are born with a certain number and size of adipose cells. Overfeeding an infant can result in an increase in the number of adipose cells as well as an increase in the size of each of these fat cells. These changes in the adipose cells are largely irreversible. Perhaps this is why some adults who have fewer and smaller fat cells can eat and eat without gaining weight, while others with more and larger fat cells can gain weight by simply "thinking about food."

Why would a mother overfeed her child? Mothers of developmentally obese children tend to be overprotective (and overfeeding). A recurring factor in these families is that either one or both of the parents view their child as a *thing,* an object, whose function it is to fulfill their needs, to compensate for failures and frustrations in their own lives. The child is often looked upon as a precious possession to whom is offered the best of everything—including the best of food (in large quantities).

The child or adolescent may also have learned that the way to cope with developmental and emotional problems is by eating, a belief that may be supported by parents through such a statement as "Eat, you'll feel better!" And since it is "not nice to talk with food in your mouth," many of the developmentally obese have never learned to express their anxieties and concerns verbally. Such inhibition of verbal expression tends to impede their emotional growth, and thus their behavior is often immature. Frequently they are withdrawn individuals with limited social involvement with the opposite sex. Hobbies are frequently sedentary in nature, such as reading, doll or stamp collecting, or watching TV. They frequently consider themselves to be ugly and often fantasize themselves as being thin, glamorous, and sexy. The concepts of self-esteem and self-importance are poor; these youngsters tend to be self-deprecating. Numerous attempts at weight reduction probably have been made—but to no avail ("It wasn't a good diet"). Such behavioral patterns are frequently explained as being caused by obesity, but obesity is *only the symptom* of unresolved emotional problems which sustain existing eating patterns.

Developmentally obese adolescents often benefit from psychological counseling concerning their personality and behavioral difficulties. A diet alone rarely works. If food, a primary source of gratification, is restricted, other kinds of rewarding experiences must be provided. If not, the adolescent's emotional problems can increase, and the diet will probably fail.

Until parents resolve the question of "How can I be a good mother [father] and deprive my [obese] child of food?" they may subconsciously sabotage the adolescent's diet. Therefore, counseling for the entire family may well be necessary.

**Reactive Obesity**/If one eats, gains weight, and becomes obese in response to a particular crisis or stress, the obesity is called "reactive." Many girls who gain excessive weight around the time of puberty, and whose weight gain seems related to sexual anxieties or sexual identification problems, fall into this category. Mothers of reactively obese adolescent girls have a particularly high incidence of difficulties with their own concepts of sexuality, and frequently sexual conflicts exist in their marriages. It is likely that these mothers instill into their daughters many of their own anxiety-laden sexual attitudes. It is no wonder then, that these girls become anxious during puberty.

Weight gain, with its accompanying sense of unfemininity, could serve to delay the adolescent girl's heterosexual involvement. Fat can be an effective buffer against the formation of sexual relationships. Obese adolescents do not have the same societal pressures for developing heterosexual behavior as do thinner ones. (We would naturally suppose that an attractive, well-developed teenager is dating; the same supposition doesn't come to mind as readily when we see a fat, blubbery adolescent.) It is important to realize that forcing a reactively obese girl into a diet regimen might only tend to increase her anxieties and may cause her to eat even more. Diets alone will not work; counseling is needed to help resolve the conflicts *that led to weight gain in the first place.*

## THE CHASTITY BELT OF OBESITY

I've often heard women say, "But a lot of men like fat women. Why, just look at those sexy European men and their fat wives." My answer to this is, "Sure, many of their wives are fat, but what about their mistresses?"

For many people, belly fat serves as a protective layer to help ensure chastity. And many men do accept their wives' obesity; it makes them less attractive and less of a sexual threat—easier to leave her at home for the day.

During adolescence, fat can also be used as an effective deterrent to heterosexual relationship and contact. A seventeen-year-old girl, who with great difficulty had lost weight from 180 to 125 pounds, came into the office and said, "You know, a funny thing is happening. I'm leaving for college next month, and all of a sudden my father is bringing home ice cream, cakes, pies, and insists on dessert with dinner. He used to be so supportive of my weight-losing. Why is he changing?"

We talked awhile . . . then she smiled . . . then she laughed and said, "Of course! He's fattening me up for college!"

She was right. Works almost as well as birth control pills. Her father, in his fears over daughter away at college, was just acting upon his own anxieties regarding her possible sexual behavior.

In thinking about why a cute, thin girl would gain weight at puberty, we must try to define the underlying psychological factors operating within her. Our country's mass advertising and "*Playboy* ethic" emphasize thinness, with its implied sexuality. We never see a fat man and a fat woman smoking cigarettes in their sports car on the way to the airport to fly off to some romantic isle. Nor has there ever been a fat nude bunny in *Playboy*. Sexuality and thinness are often regarded as inseparable. It is no wonder, therefore, that if a thin adolescent has unresolved conflicts about her emerging sexuality—usually based upon long-standing familial attitudes—her anxieties could lead her to gain weight. The weight gain to relative unattractiveness could serve to delay heterosexual involvement and, in essence, "buy time" in which to work out conflicts about sexual feelings.

Two case histories illustrate this point:

Seventeen-year-old Marcia had gained fifty pounds at age fifteen. Before her weight gain she had looked just like her sister, who was a year older. Her sister, at age sixteen, had become pregnant out of wedlock and was the talk of the local high school and small town. Coincident with her sister's pregnancy, Marcia had begun to gain weight. She was well aware of the inevitable comparisons that people would make between her and her sister's sexual activities, and wanted to make certain that no one would ever confuse her with her thin, pretty sister. She also had fears that the same thing (pregnancy) would happen to her if she continued to look like her sister. Her weight gain to obesity served the dual purpose of: (1) making her look different from her sister; and (2) creating a body mass which would be less attractive to boys.

Donna, a girl of sixteen, had begun to gain weight at age eleven, with the onset of puberty. She had developed early and had very large breasts. Donna was terrified by adolescent boys' fascination with her body and their eagerness to explore her with their hands. Her father "fed" such anxieties by pointing out to his friends his daughter's mammary development. Her mother remained silent (I don't know why). During counseling, Donna revealed fears that she would not be able to control her impulses and might turn into a nymphomaniac. She was a classic product of mass advertising and equated her thinness and big breasts with being someone who was *expected* to act out sexually. Her weight gain made her look unattractive, and the boys soon stopped their grabbing. She was more comfortable in her fatness but still ambivalent in her feelings, for she really didn't want to be fat. Yet, anytime someone would mention to her, "My, you'd be so cute if you lost weight," she would panic and put on a few more *insurance pounds*. Numerous diets had failed, and *only* after her emotional conflicts began to unravel could she lose weight with comfort.

Psychosexual problems frequently underlie significant weight gain in a pubescent girl. Usually such emotional difficulties are not first formed during pubescence, but are the result of long-standing anxieties instilled by her family or by society. If you have an adolescent who is starting to gain weight, you must examine your own behavior and sexual attitudes and assess how these may have influenced your adolescent's psychosexual development. "The way kids get even with their parents is by being like them" again holds true.

Pubertal development and emotional development may or may not occur simultaneously. Pubertal changes can occur while one still functions in a childlike manner and is emotionally immature. Or one may be emotionally mature at the advent of pubescence. The changes of puberty do not cause the individual to "grow up." The physical and sexual changes which accompany puberty do increase one's emotional anxieties and do pose adjustment problems; reactive obesity as a coping mechanism, however, indicates deeply rooted difficulties.

## ANOREXIA NERVOSA

*Anorexia nervosa* is an extremely serious medical and psychiatric disorder in which the adolescent refuses to eat adequately and is preoccupied with being thin. Such self-starvation can lead to malnutrition and, eventually, to death. Anorexia occurs predominantly in adolescents who were "perfect children." Parents may have set extremely high standards of achievement, standards that the adolescent finds impossible to maintain. Having failed as a "perfect child," she may punish herself—and her parents, for setting such high standards and expecting perfection—through self-starvation. Anorexics suffer from a deep sense of ineffectiveness, and their relentless pursuit of thinness represents an effort to feel in control of their lives and to be special. Their fetish for physical fitness is another indication of their concern over body image. Also, anorexics do not regard their emaciated appearance as either unhealthy or unattractive.

In summary, anorexia nervosa is a deeply rooted and

complicated condition—an illness derived from long-standing personal and family problems. In anorexia, as in developmental and reactive obesity, food is used to indicate underlying problems. Professional help is *always* required.

## WEIGHT LOSS

Too often, weight loss alone is overstressed in obese adolescents. After all, the ultimate goal is to improve the quality of the adolescent's life. If significant emotional problems exist, they may have to be resolved before weight loss can occur. For some adolescents, this might require only a brief time; in others, it may take years.

The obese adolescent male is seldom very interested in losing weight; he tends to be more socially acceptable than an obese female. Peers frequently equate his size with power and strength, and football and wrestling coaches often want to convert that fat into muscle. Adolescent males usually have constitutional or developmental obesity; only a very small percentage are reactively obese. Thus it is more difficult for males to lose weight, since they may have little motivation to do so and the problems leading to their weight gain may be long-standing and deeply rooted.

## WAYS PARENTS CAN HELP THEIR ADOLESCENT TO LOSE WEIGHT

1. *The adolescent must be self-motivated to lose weight.*

An absolute prerequisite for successful dieting is the adolescent's *self*-motivation to lose weight. Frequently parents will *insist* that their adolescent lose weight. If she does not want to, the diet will inevitably fail. A parent's attempt to control an adolescent's food intake usually results in the teenager's sneaking food or lying about her diet. Since what an adolescent eats is not under parental control, the teenager must be self-motivated to lose weight and to adhere to a diet.

2. *The diet must be the adolescent's "own thing."*

Since it's up to the adolescent anyway, let her take the *responsibility* for the diet. Acceptance of responsibility for the diet may increase the teenager's self-reliance and self-confidence ("My parents have enough respect and confidence in me to let me manage my own diet"). If she gains or loses weight, she must realize that it's her *own* doing. A parent doesn't want credit if the diet succeeds, nor blame if the diet fails. The adolescent must accept her own vital role in the success or failure of the diet and recognize that the outcome is up to her and not outside forces (parents, doctors, Weight Watchers, etc.)

3. *Food should not be used as a manipulative device.*

The eating of food is often used as a manipulative device between adolescent and parent; overeating can be used to anger parents. An obese adolescent may have discovered that a good way to "shake up" her parents is to walk by them while eating a candy bar. Parents should determine whether such manipulation is taking place and, if it is, stop it by not reacting to the adolescent's eating.

If an adolescent is motivated to lose weight and it's her "own thing," then parents must acknowledge her decision and stay out of it. No more: "Why did you go to the refrigerator?" "Don't you know that's fattening?" or "Is that on your diet?" All too often we, as parents, get too involved in what goes into our adolescent's mouths. If a teenager decides to go on a diet and accepts its responsibilities, then we must stop nagging about her food intake and leave the diet up to her, as if she were an adult. Being on a diet is an adultlike responsibility; parents should support their adolescent in this endeavor. Don't become a *refrigerator watchdog.*

4. *Set very limited weight-loss goals.*

Most diets are doomed to failure before they begin. An adolescent usually starts off on a diet by asking herself, or by having someone ask her: "How much would you like to lose?" Doomed.

Initiating a diet by establishing an end-point goal is really missing the boat; it does not take into account *why* the weight was gained in the first place. If a teenage girl gained weight because of sexual anxieties (reactive obesity), the goal of a "Coke-bottle-looking" figure could be subconsciously quite frightening. For example, Donna, the girl discussed earlier, who felt that if she were thin she would not be able to control her impulses and might become a nymphomaniac, would almost certainly panic if she approached the "Coke-bottle figure" goal and would then eat to regain "insurance pounds." If she weighed 185 pounds and had a goal of 115, even a loss to 180 could be interpreted as nearing the "feared" weight. However, if the initial goal were 180, she could readily achieve it, see that her fears were not realized at that weight, feel emotionally comfortable, and then plan on a goal of 175, and so on. In a rapid weight-loss situation, she would probably become frightened or anxious, and the weight would rebound. Perhaps this is why crash diets fail. Many adolescents who maintain weight loss do so only after a gradual loss.

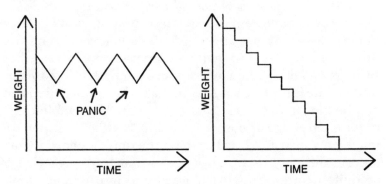

It's almost as if one's "physical" weight and "emotional" weight must have time to equilibrate before further weight loss can take place.

**5.** *Plan the diet in a positive way.*

In planning a diet, one should focus on all the foods that *can* be eaten and not on those that are *forbidden*. To be reminded of all the foods you *cannot* eat is frustrating and represents negative thinking. Positive thinking is to consider all the foods you *can* eat. Just think of all the goodies you can munch on—even if it's a big carrot or a head of lettuce. No sense in constantly reminding yourself of the evils of ice cream, cake, and potato chips. Think positive!

**6.** *A diet should satisfy your adolescent's food preferences and eating patterns.*

A diet *must* satisfy an adolescent's food preferences and eating patterns. Some like a large breakfast; others, a large lunch or dinner. Many would like an afternoon or bedtime snack fitted into their diets. It's hard enough to diet; changing one's eating patterns makes it even more difficult. Have the adolescent design her *own* diet, then discuss with her the amount of calories or carbohydrates in the diet and, if need be, suggest alternatives.

*No one specific diet is best.* An adolescent should investigate various diets and choose the one most palatable and acceptable. A diet works only if you stick to it.

**7.** *Remain supportive of your adolescent's desire to lose weight.*

If your adolescent doesn't lose weight, don't take it personally—don't get angry. It's the adolescent who's not losing weight, and your getting angry will only increase her feelings of failure. Remain supportive of her *desire* to lose weight. She is the one who has to make the ultimate decision of whether or not to eat that candy bar. Most adolescents require parental support for sticking to a diet. Supportive statements such as: "I realize that sometimes it's hard to stay on your diet" or "I see that you're sticking to your diet" may be quite helpful. Support her *desire* to lose weight; don't chastise her if she breaks the diet.

8. *Encourage your adolescent to participate in peer group activities.*

The way in which adolescents see themselves depends largely on peer group attitudes and peer group acceptance. Since obese adolescents tend to have low self-esteem and limited social involvement, their successful participation in peer group activities can improve their self-images and socialization skills. Therefore, parents can be very helpful by determining what their adolescent is good at or likes to do, and then gently encouraging her to participate in these activities with other teenagers.

*Summary*    Obesity is frequently an indication of underlying emotional difficulties. Not all obese adolescents have emotional problems, but many do. If you can determine that the obesity is constitutional, developmental, or reactive, if you have begun to understand why the weight was gained and why it is being maintained, then it may well be possible for you to help your adolescent achieve weight loss, and improve her—or his—quality of life.

# 6

# Adolescent Sexuality

A sexual revolution *has* taken place, but a fact frequently overlooked is that the revolution was initiated by the parents and grandparents of today's adolescents and not by the adolescents themselves. By far the greater percentage increase in premarital intercourse occurred between the teenage years of today's parents and grandparents than between the teenage years of today's parents and their children.

## WOMEN ENGAGING IN PREMARITAL INTERCOURSE PRIOR TO 18 YEARS OF AGE

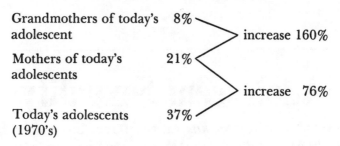

| | | |
|---|---|---|
| Grandmothers of today's adolescent | 8% | increase 160% |
| Mothers of today's adolescents | 21% | |
| | | increase 76% |
| Today's adolescents (1970's) | 37% | |

Yes, Virginia, your mother and grandmother probably knew people who engaged in premarital intercourse (or did it themselves).

The most significant recent change in sexual patterns has been the increased number of college youth who engage in premarital intercourse:

## PERCENTAGE OF PREMARITAL INTERCOURSE IN COLLEGE YOUTH BY AGE 21

| | *1950* | *early 1970's* | *mid 1970's (estimate)* |
|---|---|---|---|
| Males | 49% | 82% | 85% |
| Females | 27% | 56% | 70% |

These overall rates may be somewhat misleading, since there are marked geographical differences in the sexual behavior of college students. Eastern, New England, and West Coast university students have a higher percentage of premarital sexual relations than do midwestern university students. Also, private "elite" schools have higher rates than state universities, which are, in turn, higher than parochial or church-related schools. (I once heard a sociologist say: "My daughter can go to any parochial school in the Midwest she chooses." When I asked about his son, he laughed and said:

". . . to a private school in New England, of course." The double standard is alive and well.)

It is reassuring that there is little evidence of increased promiscuity among the majority of today's adolescents and youth. Among college males, 70 percent of those reporting to have intercourse are doing so with only one partner, and most state that a close emotional relationship exists with the sexual partner. Of college females reporting intercourse, 80 percent stated that they were involved with one partner with whom they were emotionally involved. Only 7 percent of girls reported ever having a "one-night stand."

There is no question that today's youth are more open about their sexual experiences and that we are thus more aware of these experiences than in the past. Grandparents and parents of today's youth who engaged in premarital sex did so with a greater sense of guilt. Today's youth just don't have the same degree of conflict and guilt as their forebears. In this regard, the mores of society have definitely changed.

But enough statistics. After all, if it's *your* adolescent who's engaging in premarital sex, it's 100 percent.

If it's an adolescent girl, parents more frequently become distraught, dismayed, and panicked; however, if it's an adolescent boy, parents more frequently think: "Let *her* mother worry" or "That's my boy!" In either situation, parents should be aware that teenagers in early and middle adolescence almost always have primarily *nonsexual* reasons for engaging in sexual intercourse.

## NONSEXUAL MOTIVATION FOR SEXUAL BEHAVIOR

The sexual act of a young adolescent is not, in most instances, one of erotic or physical pleasure. Nonsexual motivations —be they to gain peer approval, to escape from home, to rebel against parents, to express hostility, to search (vainly) for love, to compensate for depression, or to signal for help—are the most frequent underlying reasons for sexual behavior. Less frequently, the adolescent may have sex out of curiosity or may engage in sexual experimentation as part of behavioral experimentation. At times, sex may be part of a close emotional relationship; such "healthier" reasons, however, are definitely few and far between in the early adolescent. For the most part, the sexual act of a young adolescent is hostile, angry, and self-destructive; it is not a demonstration of caring, sharing, or feeling.

A young girl who feels that the only way she can relate to boys is with her body (nonsexual motivation) is a girl in emotional pain; she must have feelings of emptiness, loneliness, worthlessness, and alienation. What causes someone to develop such painful feelings?

Arguments supporting each of the nonsexual motivations (peer pressure, escape, rebellion, hostility, depression) as the basis of sexual acting-out can be made, but all are reflective of the adolescent's underlying problem: primarily, a perception of *missing parental concern*. A belief that parental concern is missing originates in previous parent-child and parent-adolescent relationships but, on occasion, may be an acute reaction to a new, seemingly overwhelming family or personal problem.

*People who like themselves just don't do things to hurt themselves.* One's basic feeling of self-worth comes primarily from one's early parent-child experiences. If a child perceives that her parents don't like her or don't consider her worthwhile, she is hard-pressed to develop a concept of self-worth or to see herself as being worth liking by others.

One is struck by the low self-esteem and minimal self-confidence of promiscuous young adolescents. They seem to achieve some gratification, not in the eroticism of sex, but in the parentlike fondling which precedes intercourse. It's as if they accept intercourse just to be fondled or held, in an attempt to compensate for missing parental concern.

When under stress, the adolescent may feel depressed and angry enough at her parents to engage in self-destructive behavior in order to "hurt" them. But the price is high: she first has to hurt herself. And if she doesn't like herself, she is more likely to hurt herself. A destructive pattern is thus begun. The following examples describe what an adolescent may subconsciously think while acting-out sexually:

**Sex for Peer Approval**/"Since I'm not really worthwhile, I don't have enough personal attributes—except my genitals—to get people [peers] to like me." (Any caring emotions shown by a sex partner are viewed with distrust.) "He likes my genitals, not me."

So the self-destructive cycle begins. She uses sex for peer acceptance, yet when acceptance is given she views it with distrust. Acceptance was not gained because of her personal attributes but by means of her body. Her skepticism about the value of such peer approval is perfectly justified.

**To Escape from Home**/"I can't stand being at home any longer. . . . But I don't have the personal attributes to get away on my own. . . . Use of my genitals and even getting pregnant are the only ways out for me."

**To Rebel Against Parents**/"I want to prove to my parents [and to myself] that I'm really an individual. . . . But I don't have enough strengths and attributes to achieve success. . . . The only way I can show them [and myself] I'm an individual is through the use of my genitals."

**To Express Hostility**/"I'm angry at my parents and want to hurt them. . . . I know it will hurt them if they know I'm having sex." An adolescent must feel extraordinarily help-less and inept in communicating with her parents if she feels she must act-out sexually just to "get even."

**To Search for Love**/Sexual acting-out can be an adolescent's desperate attempt to find someone to love her. Love based on genital accessibility can never last without other binding emotional ties. And what sort of a "worthwhile" individual could form a lasting, deep, and binding relationship with an empty, depressed, lonely, self-denigrating partner?

**To Combat Depression**/One way adolescents attempt to manage depression is through sexual acting-out. They may try to block out depressive feelings through a behavior that helps them to "forget" the problem, at least temporarily. Immersion in sexual acting-out can give feelings of "accep-tance," "being desirable," and "being wanted" and can blunt the underlying pain. It does not remedy the situation, how-ever, and sooner or later the unresolved problems will again emerge.

**To Signal for Help**/"My parents pay so little attention to me that only by sexual acting-out can I let them know I have problems and am in emotional pain."

**Summary of Nonsexual Motivation**/*Most adolescent sexual behavior is just an indicator of underlying emotional problems.* Such behavior should be interpreted as a cry for help from a troubled adolescent, and should be responded to accord-ingly.

As the adolescent becomes older and matures, sexual activity certainly can be *part* of a deeply rooted and binding emotional relationship. But sex is not the primary bond, the primary mechanism by which one relates to a partner. No one has ever proven that premarital intercourse, when it is truly part of a broader emotional relationship, is harmful to one's future life. It's just that only a very, very few *young* adolescents are capable of perceiving sexuality as but one component part of a relationship. Therefore, we should always be concerned about any *young* adolescent who engages in sexual activities; we should determine the basis for the behavior.

For a few adolescents, sex can be healthy, rewarding, and an integral part of their emotional growth. For most, it is a cry for help.

## WHAT TO DO IF YOU DISCOVER THAT YOUR ADOLESCENT IS HAVING SEX

When parents first discover that their teenage girl is having sexual relations, neither written nor spoken word will prevent most of them from *initially* feeling distraught, angry, hurt, bewildered, or depressed. It is unrealistic to expect many parents to remain calm and to be able to discuss the situation in a rational manner. Most parents will feel or say: "After all we've done for you, how could you do this to us? Don't you know this could ruin us? What will people think? It will just kill your poor mother[father]!"—etc. Such statements reflect the parents' initial concern for their own well-being and self-esteem rather than the eventual concern they will (hopefully) feel for their teenager. But parents are human and, like all of us, their initial reaction to stress is usually self-centered and self-defensive. In time, however, parents should be able to view the problem in a more composed and compassionate manner.

What should you, as a parent, do? First, you should try to determine whether your adolescent's motivation for sex was *sexual experimentation* as part of behavioral experimentation, was *part of an existing close emotional relationship,* or was a *self-destructive act*—a cry for help. The following three cases illustrate the differences:

*Case 1:* I recall a thirteen-year-old girl who was the top student in her grade and very inquisitive about almost all matters. During an office visit, she said: "You know, I've heard and read so much about sex, I wanted to give it a try. There was this fifteen-year-old guy I know, so we decided to do it. You know, he was more scared than I was. Well, we did it. It wasn't at all what I expected; in fact, I really didn't even enjoy it. It was so physical. I felt [emotionally] so little. You know, I don't think I'm going to do it again until I really like someone, maybe even wait till I'm married." (My pipe almost fell out of my mouth as this thirteen-year-old related her experience in a most poised, insightful, and mature manner.)

*Sexual experimentation* here was part of behavioral experimentation—she had not used sex in a destructive or manipulative way. However, if her parents had found out, acute frenzy would probably have been immediate and, I'm certain, neither necessary nor constructive.

*Case 2:* D.J. was seventeen years old and had been "going with" her eighteen-year-old boyfriend for the past three years. She wore his high school ring and he, her locket. He was attending the same local college she planned to attend. They had a close emotional relationship and talked of future marriage. They were both responsible, sensitive people. They had avoided intercourse until they "felt ready." She came into the office and asked for birth control pills to protect herself from pregnancy.

They had a close emotional relationship and had decided to include *sex as part of their emotional involvement.*

*Case 3:* T.V. was fourteen and from an affluent physician's family. Her schoolwork was deteriorating and she came in to the office fearing that she had venereal disease. One week before her visit she had had intercourse with six boys from her school's basketball team. In the past six months or so she had had intercourse with at least eleven other boys. (I was struck by the ease with which she related her involvements and could just feel her underlying anger and hostility.) I had seen her a year before, when she related that things were going well for her. I believe she knew that I would now involve her parents—not because she was now sexually promiscuous, but because she was having problems, problems that were probably family-based.

Her parents were quite reluctant to admit that their "little girl" had any problems and were even more hesitant about reviewing their own parenting behaviors and family dynamics. After initially berating their daughter and threatening to send her away to boarding school, they finally admitted that they were thinking of getting a divorce. They didn't think that their daughter was aware of their problems (children always are). The daughter's sexual behavior represented an attempt to tell her parents that she was distraught and frightened by the possibility of their divorcing. By forcing her parents to focus their attention on *her* problems rather than on *theirs,* she might draw them close again. *A cry for help*—for the entire family.

Parents should neither berate nor reject their adolescent because of sexual acting-out. Since it was probably nonsexually motivated and largely based upon family problems to begin with, further parental rejection or abandonment will only foster additional sexual acting-out and will not diminish the underlying (nonsexual) motivation. Parents will inevitably have to face their own roles in the situation.

If your adolescent is promiscuous, the question of "Where did we go wrong?" is appropriate and needs to be addressed. Review of parent-child and parent-adolescent relationships is often painful but must be made. The purpose of this review is *not*—*NOT*—to place blame or to adjudicate guilt, but is to understand how the problems started, how the difficulties grew, and why they have not been solved.

*It's never just the parents. It's never just the teenager.* Both parents and teenager must be motivated and willing to work together to resolve their differences.

Dysparenting, or missing parental love, may not be the result of deliberate or conscious neglect by parents. They may be genuinely unaware of the needs of their children, or unaware of how they might fill them. If one is unaware, one is inattentive, and such "inattentiveness" may be misconstrued by the child to mean "uncaring." To a child (as well as to an adolescent), the belief that one's parents are uncaring may lead to feelings of being *unworthy* of care, with a resultant loss of self-esteem. Such feelings predispose the teenager, when angry at her parents, to act-out in self-destructive ways (sexually) and to hurt herself in order to hurt her parents. An alternative method for an adolescent to express anger is by quite simply telling her parents that she's angry at them and why she feels that way. What usually prevents the teenager from engaging in such a direct and healthy confrontation is the belief that her parents don't really care what she feels. In such a situation, the teenager has little recourse but to act-out.

If an adult becomes angry and feels that another won't listen—since the adult is independent and not dependent upon the other—the adult can simply walk away from the situation. The adolescent doesn't have such a luxury. An adolescent is dependent upon parents and cannot leave so easily. Acting-out, in order to get parents to listen, may be the only existing alternative.

Parents and teenager together must identify the problems in their relationship in order to resolve them. The situation can get better, can turn around, and the home can become a happier place for all. What should *never* happen is for parents to say: "It's your life ... do with it what you want." This is a very cold and distant and uncaring response by a parent. Yes, it's true that teenagers are capable of making their own decisions about many things, but parents should realize that the teenager's motivations for sex are usually nonsexual in origin and stem from unresolved family discord. Parents' statements that seem to indicate that they don't care will only alienate the adolescent further and reinforce the unhealthy behavior.

I recall vividly an instance in which a sexually promiscuous young teenager sobbed: "Why didn't they tell me to stop? I didn't want them to tell me to get birth control pills! I wanted them to tell me to stop— to *care enough about me* to tell me to stop!" The girl had set up a test of parental love: She let them find out about her behavior to see whether they loved her enough to stop her from continuing it. In this instance, her most terrifying fear was realized—her parents really didn't care about her. They failed the test.

Professional intervention—by a doctor, a nurse, a psychologist, a social worker, a counselor, a clergyman, etc.—is indicated if parents and teenager cannot resolve their differences by themselves. Often parents and teenagers are just too angry to communicate further. Professional assistance can decrease the tensions, restore communication, and help the family work out their differences. Promiscuity is a cry for help—a cry that must not go unheeded.

## Summary of What to Do

1. If you discover that your teenager is having sex, don't blow your top. Stop and *think*.
2. Differentiate between sexual experimentation, sex as part of an emotional relationship, and self-destructive sexual behavior (a cry for help!).
3. Look for the underlying motivation for the behavior; try not to react to the behavior alone.
4. If the adolescent is promiscuous, review your parent/child and parent/teenager relationships. It's never just the adolescent. It's never just the parent.
5. Professional help is indicated when differences between you and your teenager cannot be resolved.

## MASTURBATION

Blindness. Insanity. Warts. Acne. Impotence. Satanic damnation. The myths and old wives' tales of the harmful results of masturbation have invoked fearful fantasies upon normal teenagers for centuries. There are *no* known harmful effects, either medical or emotional, resulting from masturbation. In fact, it is more of a tension-reducing activity than a sexual one.

Surveys have shown that over 80 percent of teenage boys and 30 percent of teenage girls masturbate. It's just as normal to masturbate as it is not to masturbate—it's up to the individual to decide.

What should parents say if they discover that their teenager is masturbating? First, don't get angry. What is there to be angry about, anyway? Masturbation, in private, doesn't imply problems, nor will it lead to problems. In reality, parents and adolescents seldom discuss masturbation; it is performed in private, and parents usually overlook evidence that it occurs. Perhaps it's better that way. There is no need for parents to determine whether their teenager masturbates. There is a need to dissipate the possible guilt feelings and apprehensions engendered by myths and fantasies about the dangers of masturbation. Parents, therefore, might be well advised simply to offer the information that many people masturbate, that it's not harmful, and that it's a matter of personal and private choice.

I remember one instance when, as part of his yearly checkup, I talked with an adolescent boy about masturbation. I didn't ask him if he did it or not (four out of five do) but approached it as follows: "There sure are a lot of myths and wives' tales about masturbation. Have you heard any?" (He gave a sheepish nod, and I continued.) "Well, that's what they are, *myths* . . . it can't hurt you, doesn't make you crazy, doesn't cause warts and the like. But it is a very private thing." (A sheepish grin now replaced the sheepish nod.) I had given him permission to think and talk about masturbation and reassurance that it wasn't harmful. I was not judgmental, just talking "man to man."

Two weeks later, the same scene was repeated with another youth.

About a week after that, a mother called and asked if I had talked to her son about masturbation. I didn't know whether she would be angry or what, but I said, "Yes, I did." She responded: "Well, I heard Fred [her son] and Bobby [his cousin, whom I had seen three weeks earlier] laughing and talking about their conversations with you . . . and it was just touching. They were talking openly about the myths of masturbation and how they now realize that they aren't true. My husband and I just couldn't bring ourselves to talk with him about it . . . we're so glad you did."

Anyone can offer such simple reassurance, which can diminish the intensity of anxiety-laden feelings and allow masturbation to be discussed in a healthy and constructive manner.

## BIG BREASTS, LITTLE BREASTS; BIG PENIS, LITTLE PENIS

Anatomy may be destiny. Sexual myths and fantasies of genital size do influence one's sexual identity, especially in the young adolescent who is just beginning to develop as a sexual person. *External values* regarding sexuality (adult values, peer group values, societal mores, mass advertising) can exert a more powerful influence on the young adolescent than *internal values* (self-esteem, ego strengths, self-identity) which are not yet fully formed and developed.

In a purely physical sense, the size of breasts does not correlate with either physical arousal or breast-feeding capability, and penile size is of little consequence for success-ful intercourse and procreation. Physically, we are more alike than different, yet *learned* emotional responses to phys-ical shape and size can have great effect on one's sexual identity.

**Big Breasts**/Girls begin puberty at various ages and differ in the amount of mammary tissue they possess. If a girl's breasts develop early or are large, this can affect her social and interpersonal relationships to a significant degree. Boys her own age may tease her unmercifully about her breasts, may merely ogle her, or may be "afraid" of her. Boys may develop hands "ten feet long and ten feet wide" and persevere in their efforts to touch and feel. The effect of all this may be to assign to the girl a sexual identity based upon the size of her breasts. To many young girls, this can be devastating. Though physically mature, a girl may be emotionally imma-ture and yet forced to think in sexual terms, even if only to protect herself. Although a maladjusted girl may urge on the boys by wearing tight sweaters (pink, of course), many large-breasted girls will try to hide their mammaries by wear-ing loose-fitting clothing, by keeping their hair long and over their chests, by becoming round-shouldered and bent at the waist, and even by gaining weight.

Just because a girl's mammary tissue grew early and in large amounts, people may fantasize that she is a *sexual object*—and *object* is the key word. She is not viewed as a person, but as an object. Since most young adolescents have not yet established their own self-identities by internal de-terminants, the strong external influences of the peer group may cause her to accept the identity of "sexual object." A growing suspicion and distrust of boys ("They don't like *me*, they like my *breasts*") may emerge. Alternatively, a young adolescent may like the boys' attention and use her breasts as the primary way she relates with them; she can gain immediate peer group acceptance by using her body to manipulate the boys. But she pays a price for this acceptance —she learns to relate with others in a physical manner rather than in an emotional, caring, and intellectual manner. When one regards the other as a sexual object and not as a complete person, with the relationship based primarily on a *physical* attraction, a long-term and satisfying *emotional* relationship is hard to achieve.

It is sad and tragic that the number of mammary cells one possesses can so often define one's sexual identity. Adult advice and assistance are necessary to help a young girl develop appropriate emotional interpersonal qualities and avoid succumbing to an externally defined identity as a sexual object.

**Little Breasts**/When a girl's breasts develop late or are small, emotional difficulties can arise: "What's wrong with me?" "Why am I different?" "If I have small breasts, will I be capable of having children?" "Will I be sexual?" Many girls with small breasts have these unspoken fears; however, many of them are outgoing and friendly with boys, perhaps because they may feel more comfortable in heterosexual relationships than do bigger-breasted girls who may have sexual-object identities. Smaller-breasted girls are not given as much of a sexual identity, and they may be less afraid of exploring hands, so they may find it easier to develop heterosexual relationships on *emotional,* rather than *physical,* bases. In the long run, relationships on an emotional basis will aid them in developing realistic and comfortable adult sexual identities.

On occasion, smaller-breasted girls develop a "reactive sexuality"; that is, they may react to their poor physical self-images by using their vaginas to prove that they are female, since they perceive their breasts as failing to present this "proof."

It makes no logical sense, nor is it right, but when we see a cute sixteen-year-old with big breasts, we consider her to be more of a sexual person than we do a cute sixteen-year-old with small breasts. The external values regarding breast size are ubiquitous and powerful in our society. Adults can help an adolescent girl avoid unnecessary emotional conflict over the size of her breasts by providing preventive, anticipatory guidance if her breast development is early or late, large or small.

**Big Penis**/A boy whose penis development begins early or who has a large penis is subjected to peer group pressures which are similar to those of a girl with large breasts. Many schools have common showers after gym class, and the early-developing or large penis "stands out like a sore thumb." For many young adolescents (and, unfortunately, for many adults as well), penis size is associated with masculinity, and the "endowed" boy may become the object of sexual-prowess fantasies by boys who have not yet developed. To the normal, sexually insecure young adolescent who is facing his own difficulties in heterosexual adjustments, the large-penised adolescent may be seen as a person who should be designated to carry forward the banner of "male sexuality" and thus be pressured into heterosexual relationships and sexual activities. "Did you get anything?" "How was it?" "Why don't you take *her* out?" "Do you have a French tickler?"—his peers ask while eagerly hanging on his every word, reported deed, or "knowing" look.

The cumulative effect of such peer group expectations may influence the manner in which he relates with girls and will probably result in his developing a primarily physical or sexual way of relating with females, often at the expense of emotional involvement. The external sources of his sexual role definition may be in direct conflict with his own internal feelings about himself and the way he wants to relate with girls; however, the strong peer group pressures often prevail. If one's physical maturity is far in advance of one's emotional maturity, severe emotional conflicts can result. Pubescent genital development correlates with an increase in overall body size and strength; therefore, the boy whose penis develops early is usually the biggest and strongest lad in his peer group. His greater size and strength, added to his peers' fantasies about his sexual capabilities, create additional pressure for the boy to be a "sexual achiever."

Parents must help such a boy to understand that his physical development doesn't mean he has to change the kind of person he wants to be, peer group pressures notwithstanding.

**Little Penis**/Perhaps the most difficult emotional situation an adolescent boy can be in is when he thinks he has a small penis. Although he may have heard of "late bloomers," may know that there is no significant size difference among mature, erect penises, and may know that a female's vaginal sensitivity is greatest in the outer third of her vagina and therefore penile length is of little importance, this knowledge is usually of limited consolation. The boy who is late in developing or who thinks he has a small penis may be quite shy, may stay away from group showers or group nudity situations, or may feel so insecure as to avoid any relationships with girls. He may go to the opposite extreme and be a braggart, an attention-seeking "acting-outer," and the one who always has the latest in pornography. In any form it takes, his behavior is generated by his feelings of inadequacy or inferiority. His poor sense of sexual identity can drastically influence the way he relates with both males and females in his peer group.

Information about normal variations in the timing of genital development, help in defining what really is "male sexuality," and supportive counseling are all important in assisting such a youngster (or adult). We must try to prevent the self-destructive behavior that so often occurs when one considers oneself to be sexually inadequate. Sexual inadequacy is almost always an emotional state, not a physical state.

## TEENAGE PREGNANCY AND ABORTION: OR QUEEN VICTORIA, WHERE ARE YOU NOW THAT WE NEED YOU?"

One out of ten girls of junior and senior high school age becomes pregnant. Until recently, teenage pregnancy was thought to be a problem confined to nonwhite, inner-city girls from lower socioeconomic groups. This is no longer the case; more and more teenage girls from *all* socioeconomic levels of society are becoming pregnant. Illegitimacy rates for middle-class girls are rising, and rates for inner-city youth appear to be falling.

Many people believed that the availability of birth control measures would decrease the pregnancy rate in teenage girls. This has not proven to be the case. Seventy percent of sexually active teenage girls who know about birth control methods and know where to get them are not using preventive measures. If one considers that, in most young teenagers, the primary motivations for sex are anger, hostility, escapism, rebellion, etc., one can understand why these girls might not seek out and use self-protective measures. If a teenager is engaged in self-destructive behavior, she seldom considers ways of making the behavior less destructive.

Some young girls simply cannot imagine themselves as able to become pregnant and therefore give no thought to contraception. Also, many young girls who are well aware of the necessity for contraceptive measures and how to obtain them may fail to do so because they believe that premarital intercourse is "wrong." If intercourse is wrong, then preparing for it (premeditation) makes it even more wrong than if it "just happens." It's no wonder that 10 percent of girls become pregnant before the age of nineteen. Very few of these girls really want to be pregnant, and many consider terminating their pregnancies: abortion.

Although abortion is now readily available in most states, this has not decreased the illegitimacy rate. Approximately 30 percent of teenage girls who are offered the opportunity to abort their pregnancies choose this option. Only 15-18 percent of teenage girls who complete their pregnancies give up their babies for adoption. Therefore, over half of pregnant teenagers will bear, keep, and raise their children.

Pregnant teenagers can have immediate and future medical and emotional problems:

*Immediate medical problems.* A teenager is at increased risk of having problems with her pregnancy, fetus, and newborn. If she receives prompt diagnosis of her pregnancy and comprehensive prenatal care, many of the dire consequences (toxemia, miscarriage, stillbirth, prematurity, newborn morbidity and mortality) of untreated teenage pregnancy can be avoided.

*Future medical problems.* Whether a teenager terminates her pregnancy by abortion or carries it to delivery, there is an increased risk that she will have serious complications in future pregnancies. In women who have had abortions as teenagers, there is a significantly higher rate for miscarriage, stillbirth, premature delivery, and newborn death when compared with women of the same age who have never had an abortion. Women who had their first child while in their early teens also have a higher incidence of prematurity and perinatal death in subsequent pregnancies. The dilemma is that, regardless of whether a teenager aborts or carries to term, she will have a significantly higher risk of problems with future pregnancies than if she had not been pregnant as a teenager. The reasons for this are not yet known; perhaps it has to do with the stretching of a possibly "immature" uterus. In any event, to help prevent possible future difficulties, the teenager should avoid getting pregnant in the first place.

*Immediate emotional problems.* Most women have fond, warm, and loving memories of the moment of discovery that they are pregnant. In my experience, informing a young adolescent that she is pregnant does not cause her to be filled with fondness, warmth, and love; most often, her reaction is one of disbelief, anger, and depression. Most sit there with blank looks on their faces and, after a few moments, their eyes well up in tears. For me, this has rarely been a sharing of the joy of a new life but a period of helping the youngster figure out what to do next: To tell her boyfriend? To tell her parents? To tell her friends? To tell the school? To abort? To continue? To bear and give up the child? To bear and keep the child? To rush into an unwanted marriage? To leave town? I've just never heard a young girl say gleefully: "That's great! I'm pregnant, and I feel beautiful!"

Harsh reality replaces fantasy. In this stressful situation, the underlying emotional problems that led to unprotected sex in the first place are brought into focus by the pregnancy and the necessity of deciding what to do about it.

The decision to abort or continue the pregnancy *must* be the girl's own, hopefully after constructive input from the family. As never before, the young girl *needs* her family and the emotional support that only they can provide at this most difficult time. Although alternatives are available, no matter which she chooses, any decision will have lifelong impact.

There are no hard-and-fast rules or guidelines that can help a youngster to make a decision regarding her pregnancy—it's a highly individualized process of thinking things through and working them out. I do feel that if the girl *ever* talks of abortion as "killing," or refers to the fetus as a "baby" (or by any other term that denotes a living being), the value of abortion must be seriously questioned. It's one thing to "terminate the pregnancy," "get rid of a *clot*," "stop *it*," "Take care of *it*"; it's quite another thing to "*kill* it," "get rid of the *baby*," or "*kill* the *baby*."

If the teenager decides to continue with the pregnancy, numerous emotional readjustments in her own life and within her family have to be made to accommodate the newborn.

*Future emotional problems.* No matter the outcome, pregnancy changes one's life. If the adolescent decides to terminate or abort her pregnancy, she may feel guilt and depression in the future. Ethical, legal, and religious issues aside, abortion does terminate a potential human being. Years later, many women reflect upon their abortions and have feelings of guilt. The abortion may be intellectualized as the proper decision at the time, but the nagging, guilt-ridden "gut" feeling of "Did I *really* do the right thing?" often arises later. Many women who aborted their first pregnancies have repeated pregnancies later on, as if to compensate for the "loss" of their aborted one. After the initial shock has worn off, a woman may have depressive feelings based upon the loss of her fetus and loss of her previous sense of well-being caused by the unwanted pregnancy.

If a teenager continues her pregnancy and eventually gives up her newborn for adoption, other emotional problems may arise. Feelings of guilt about "abandoning" her baby, with subsequent frantic searches for her offspring, are not uncommon. Again, though a woman can rationalize an adoptive placement at the time, she may later be plagued with doubts as to the wisdom of her choice.

If she continues the pregnancy and keeps her baby, numerous emotional adjustments must be made, both within herself and with her family. The adolescent wants independence, but she needs assistance in caring for the newborn. This often places her back into a more dependent position within her family. Despite an increased liberalization of society's attitudes regarding illegitimacy, the adolescent unwed mother is still socially stigmatized. Latent feelings of anger toward her baby ("How could he do this to me?") frequently develop and must be resolved. If the teenager abdicates her mothering role to her parents or others in her family, problems will arise when the teenager becomes older, is capable of effective parenting, wants to raise the child, and starts to "reclaim" the child from surrogate parents.

## METHODS OF CONTRACEPTION

**Abstinence**/No pregnancy, no risks, no side effects, no cost, no contraindications result from abstinence. If an adolescent herself decides on this method, the likelihood of her adhering to it is quite good. If, however, she is pressured into such a decision by parents, family, school, or religion, the failure rate is quite high.

**Birth Control Pills**/There are two types of birth control pills: "sequential" pills and "combination" pills. Sequential pills come in sets which for the first fourteen to fifteen days of the cycle contain only estrogen, but for the next five to six days contain both an estrogen and a progestogen. Use of sequential pills has been discontinued for the most part because of their side effects. Combination pills are the ones more frequently prescribed. They contain both an estrogen and a progestogen, and all the pills in the twenty- or twenty-one-day packages are the same. The twenty-eight-day packages include twenty-one hormone tablets plus seven iron tablets, since for many women it's easier to remember to take a pill *every* day than to take a pill daily for three weeks, stop for a week, and remember when to start again.

Before starting the pill, all women should have a breast and pelvic examination and a Papanicolaou or "Pap" smear.

These should be repeated yearly. The best way to start birth control pills is to take the first one on the *fifth day of menstruation,* counting the first day of flow as Day One.

The advantages of the pill are that they are easy to take and very effective, if taken as prescribed. Smaller amounts of estrogen are used now than when the pill was first introduced; therefore, side effects are probably fewer and milder now. For a teenager, the major pitfall in the use of the pill is that she has to remember to take them—and this requires *motivation!* Even though the adolescent may be aware that the pill must be taken daily, this does not ensure that she will be motivated to do so. In general, the older and emotionally mature adolescent is more likely to take the pill as prescribed. In many clinics, the birth rate is quite high for young adolescents "supposedly" on the pill. A frequently stated statistic is: "One out of every three adolescents fails to take the pill as directed."

Birth control pills work by: inhibiting ovulation, blocking the release of gonadotrophic hormones from the pituitary gland, altering the normal monthly maturation of the lining of the uterus (the endometrium), and changing the cervical mucus so that it's more difficult for the sperm to enter the uterus.

Contraindications to an adolescent's use of the pill are the same as for an adult. They include: (1) thrombophlebitis or thromboembolic disorders, cerebral apoplexy (stroke), or a past history of these conditions; (2) liver disease; (3) undiagnosed abnormal vaginal bleeding; (4) known or suspected estrogen-dependent tumors. If the girl has a history of migraine, hypertension, or diabetes, careful individual management by the physician is required.

Adolescents are often quite concerned about side effects caused by the pill. Certain side effects are due to estrogen and others to progestogen. Some birth control pills are estrogen-dominant; others are progestogen-dominant. In selecting an oral contraceptive for an individual, a doctor will consider her constitutional makeup and medical history, then prescribe the combination he thinks will suit her best.

### Estrogen-Produced Side Effects

Fluid retention—there may be a cyclic weight gain.

Headaches—migraine or other headaches may occur.

Gastrointestinal problems—"upset stomach" and/or a "bloated" feeling may occur.

Breast tenderness and swelling—breasts may become somewhat enlarged and occasionally uncomfortable.

Hypertension—there may be an increase in blood pressure.

Painful periods—menstrual pain may be increased with estrogen-dominant pills.

Increased menstrual flow—this is related to the degree of estrogen dominance.

### Progestogen-Induced Side Effects

Decreased or absent menstrual periods—the endometrium may become scanty, causing decreased or absent periods.

Acne—acne tends to get worse on progestogen-dominant pills.

Weight gain and increased appetite—true weight gain can occur. This is different from the fluid retention associated with estrogens.

Monilial vaginitis—progestogens seem to make the vaginal mucosa more susceptible to monilia.

Alopecia—loss of hair, a rare side effect.

Depression—perhaps more frequent on progestogen-dominant pills.

Breasts may become slightly smaller.

Early-cycle spotting or "breakthrough" bleeding—bleeding between menstrual periods.

Therefore, by taking into account the effects of the estrogens and progestogens, we can gain certain advantages by using a pill in which one or the other is dominant.

*Instances Where Estrogen-Dominant Pills May Be Preferred*

To improve acne.
To enlarge small breasts.
To correct scanty or absent menstrual periods.
To stop spotting between periods.
To diminish appetite.
To decrease the recurrence of monilial vaginitis.

*Instances Where Progestogen-Dominant Pills May Be Preferred*

To diminish nausea or bloating.
To decrease cyclic tenderness in fibrocystic disease of the breasts.
To lessen premenstrual weight gain (from fluid retention).
To relieve premenstrual tension.
To alleviate painful periods.
To decrease heavy menstrual flow.

This is not meant to be an all-inclusive discussion of the medical risks and side effects of birth control pills. That is best left to your physician.

**Intrauterine Device (IUD)**/IUDs are small plastic or metal devices that are inserted into the uterine cavity. It is not exactly known how IUDs work—by interfering with the sperm, or egg, or most probably by acting as a "foreign body" which stimulates the lining of the uterus so as to prevent implantation of the fertilized egg.

In general, girls who have not been pregnant have a harder time with IUDs (cramps, bleeding, expulsion of the IUD, pelvic pain) than girls who have been pregnant. However, recent advances in IUD design may diminish this factor. In some clinics, IUDs are preferred, for although they're only 95 percent effective, one doesn't have to worry about taking a birth control pill every day. In adolescents, overall pregnancy rates are lower with IUDs than with birth control pills. IUDs are not 100 percent effective because they can be expelled (come out) without the wearer being aware of it; or, on occasion, pregnancy can result even with the IUD in place. Strings or beads attached to the intrauterine part of the device protrude through the cervix and into the vaginal canal. One can tell whether the IUD is in place by checking for the presence of these beads or strings.

### Advantages of an IUD

No concern over effects of the hormones in birth control pills.
No need to remember to take pills daily.
Protection is always present.
Can be removed easily by a doctor or nurse.
Can be used if medical contraindications exist for the pill.

### Disadvantages of an IUD

Cramping, bleeding, or pelvic pain may occur.
May be expelled without the user's knowledge.
Pregnancy is possible even with the IUD in place (2 to 5 percent chance).
Should not be inserted if pelvic or genital infection is present.
Cannot be used in various types of cervical or uterine abnormalities.
May increase the risk of uterine infection.
Slight risk of uterine perforation.

**Diaphragms**/Diaphragms can be an effective contraceptive, but they should *never be used alone*. Diaphragms must be used in combination with spermicidal jelly or foam. Side effects caused by diaphragms are practically nonexistent.

Diaphragms have to be fitted by a health professional to ensure that the cervix will be covered properly. Different people will need different sizes for a perfect fit. The diaphragm of today is quite similar to the original one designed in 1882. It is made of thin, soft rubber and is shaped like a bowl, with a flexible metal spring within the rim. Application is by squeezing the diaphragm's rims together, inserting it in the vagina and over the cervix, and then allowing it to spring back into shape. When properly fitted, the device will cover the cervix and fit between the back wall of the vagina and the pubic bone. It is not felt during intercourse.

The diaphragm must *always* be used with a spermicidal cream or jelly. Used alone, the diaphragm is no match for the millions of sperm swimming around it. The spermicide (sperm-killing medication) is applied all around the rim of the diaphragm. If the diaphragm and spermicide are inserted more than a half hour prior to intercourse, more spermicide should be added immediately before intercourse, without removing the diaphragm. Following intercourse, the diaphragm should be left in place for at least eight hours, and it's important not to douche for eight hours—this would only wash away the spermicide. If intercourse is repeated within the eight hours, more cream or jelly must be inserted and, again, the diaphragm must not be removed until eight more hours have passed.

## Advantages of the Diaphragm

Few, if any, side effects (most are due to the jelly or cream rather than to the diaphragm itself).
Used only when needed.
Relatively easy to use.

## Disadvantages of the Diaphragm

Must be properly fitted by a health professional.
Requires advance planning. The adolescent must be motivated to plan ahead and properly prepare for intercourse. This is quite difficult for many teenagers (and adults).
A spermicidal jelly or foam must be used as well.
Diaphragms can slip off the cervix.
It must be left in place for eight hours after intercourse.

**Condoms**/Condoms ("rubbers") are more effective in the prevention of venereal disease than they are in the prevention of pregnancy. As with the diaphragm, the condom *must* be used in conjunction with other contraceptives, such as a diaphragm and/or spermicides.

The condom is made from thin rubber and is placed over the erect penis just before intercourse. It prevents sperm from entering the vagina. Since the quality of condoms is controlled by the Food and Drug Administration, one brand is as effective as another and breakage is rare. Failure of the condom in preventing pregnancy is attributed to inconsistent use, tearing of the rubber if it becomes too dry, or tearing because no room was left at the tip to collect the semen (one-half to one inch should be left). Problems can be avoided by using prelubricated condoms or by applying a spermicide around the outside of the condom. To ensure that the condom doesn't slip off during withdrawal, it should be held in place.

*Advantages of the Condom*

> The male is involved in planning for contraception.
> Protection against transmission of venereal disease (both giving and receiving).
> No prescription is necessary.
> Readily available and inexpensive.
> No side effects or risks.

*Disadvantages of the Condom*

> One has to be motivated to interrupt foreplay and apply the condom over an erection.
> It has to be used consistently.
> Some males say it dulls sensation.
> Some women don't like the way it feels.
> Must be used in conjunction with another agent, such as a diaphragm or spermicide.

**Spermicidal Foams, Jellies, and Creams**/The concept of placing a material in the vagina to prevent pregnancy is recorded as early as 1900 B.C. Recent developments have made the spermicides effective and safe to use. Since foam is more highly dispersed in the vagina than jellies or creams, it is more effective. Also, a foam base forms a better barrier to block the sperm from reaching the cervix. Spermicides should *definitely be used with other contraceptive agents.* Use of a condom or a diaphragm with the spermicide is twice as protective.

The foam is inserted into the vagina with an applicator. It should be inserted thirty to sixty minutes prior to intercourse. If intercourse is repeated, additional foam must be inserted. *Don't douche*—that will only dilute and wash out the spermicide.

Creams and jellies are messier to use, may leak out, and don't disperse as well as the foam. The least effective spermicides are vaginal suppositories and foaming tablets —there is a fifteen-minute waiting period and a risk that they might not dissolve completely.

If the spermicide irritates the skin, another brand should be used.

*Advantages of Spermicides*

>Readily available and inexpensive.
>Easy to use.
>No side effects or risks.
>No prescription is necessary.

*Disadvantages of Spermicides*

>Should be used in conjunction with another contraceptive
>    —diaphragm or condom.
>Requires planning and use prior to intercourse.

**Rhythm**/The rhythm method is based upon the fact that women can become pregnant only during and shortly after ovulation. It is assumed that ova are available for fertilization for only twenty-four hours and that sperm remains viable for forty-eight hours. Therefore, theoretically, there are only three days in each menstrual cycle when conception is possible. However, ova may be available for up to three days, and some hearty sperm may live for five to six days—a total of up to nine days during which fertilization is possible. In addition, it is difficult to predict exactly when ovulation will occur, particularly in adolescents. Depending on circumstances, it is possible to conceive at *any* time during the menstrual cycle.

*Rhythm is not a contraceptive method that an adolescent can use with any degree of confidence or safety.*

*Advantages of Rhythm*

May be slightly better than nothing at all.

*Disadvantages of Rhythm*

Cannot be relied upon as a preventive technique.


## After Unprotected Intercourse . . .

| *"Morning after"* | | *Cost* |
|---|---|---|
| Diethylstilbestrol | (frequently one needs an antinausea preparation as well) | $ 2–3 |
| *"Week after"* | | |
| Suction curettage | | $ 50–150 |
| *"Month after"* | | |
| Dilation and curettage | | $200–500 |

*"Am I pregnant?"*

1. Urine tests for pregnancy will not become positive for at least twenty-eight days after conception or forty-four days after the first day of the last menstrual period. False-positive urine tests may be caused by a large list of drugs (for example, but not all-inclusive: aspirin, phenobarbital, and many of the tranquilizers) and by protein in the urine.
2. Progesterone may be prescribed to see whether menses can be induced. Progesterone usually does not promote menses in a woman who is pregnant.

## CONTRACEPTIVE MYTHS OF ADOLESCENTS

*"It's absolutely safe to have intercourse during the period."*

Many adolescents have very irregular periods, and it's possible for ovulation to occur at any time, even during a time of vaginal bleeding.

### Pull-out or withdrawal

"No deposit, no return" is a myth. By the time the male perceives ejaculation to be imminent, some sperm will have already escaped into the vagina. It takes only one sperm to fertilize an egg. Good intentions are not enough.

### Douching

Douching is *not* a method of birth control. There is almost as much chance of washing the sperm closer to the cervix as of washing them away. Since a sperm can reach the cervix in under two minutes (speedy little devils!), even a mad dash to the bidet is usually futile.

Douching isn't really necessary for hygienic purposes. Vaginal secretions do a good job in cleansing. Douching can cause irritation, upset the normal vaginal flora, and can pre-

## CONTRACEPTIVE AGENTS

| Agent | Estimated Pregnancy Rate Per 100 Woman Years | Risks/Side Effects | Medical Contra-indications | Approximate Cost |
|---|---|---|---|---|
| Abstinence | 0 | None | None | $ 0.00 |
| Birth control pills | 0.1 | Thromboemboli, weight gain, fluid retention, headache, nausea | Previous thrombo-embolism, liver or cardiovascular disease, migraine headaches, suspected breast cancer | $2.00/month |
| Intrauterine device | 5 | Perforation of uterus, cramps, irregular bleeding | Uterine abnormalities or problems, infection | $20–40 and up |
| Diaphragm and spermicidal jelly | 8 | Rare sensitivity to latex or spermicide | None | $7–10/month |
| Condoms | 14 | None | None | $2.50/dozen |
| Spermicides | 10–20 | Occasional sensitivity | None | $2.50/can |
| Rhythm | 14–38 | None (except pregnancy) | None | $0.00 |
| None usually | 80 | None | None | Doctor and |

dispose one to infection. A bath or shower works as well as the vaginal deodorants, which are not necessary and can be harmful.

## VENEREAL DISEASE

One can be infected with VD without having any symptoms.
VD can be cured if it is treated early enough.
The treatment of VD is by prescription drugs only. There is no self-treatment or product sold over the counter in drugstores that can cure VD.
VD can be acquired over and over again.
VD can kill you.
Birth control pills neither prevent nor treat VD.
VD endangers not only the infected person but all people with whom the infected person has intimate contact.
A pregnant woman with *untreated* VD may pass it on to her fetus, often with devastating consequences to the fetus.
VD is not a disease of dirt or filth, but of sexual activity.
The diagnosis and treatment of VD is confidential information.
Not all vaginal or penile discharges are caused by VD.

### Gonorrhea

Gonorrhea has been a frequent complication of lovemaking throughout the ages. In the Old Testament Book of Leviticus, gonorrhea is described in detail.

The gonococcus, the bacterium that causes gonorrhea, lives for only a few seconds outside the human body. It is therefore almost impossible to catch it from a toilet seat, towel, cups, plates, etc., that have previously been used by an infected person. The bacteria live in warm, moist mucous membranes (vagina, cervix, urethra, mouth, throat, anus), and the common feature of intimate contact is that the two people's mucous membranes are brought together. If your partner has gonorrhea, there is about a fifty-fifty chance of catching it during sex.

### Gonorrhea in the male

**Early symptoms**/Most males who have gonorrhea of the penile urethra (tube that runs from the bladder and through the penis) first notice symptoms three to five days after intercourse. However, symptoms can appear as soon as one day or as long as two weeks after infestation. At first, a clear, thin discharge comes out of the penis, and then it gets thicker and usually becomes yellow or yellowish-green. Urination may hurt or burn, often quite severely, and the urine may be bloody. The lymph nodes in the groin may become enlarged and tender.

In general, the male is "lucky"—anyone with a penile discharge and burning on urination will know that something is wrong and (hopefully) seek medical advice. What is happening more and more, however, is that a male may not have any symptoms with the infection and thus may not seek medical help. He is still infected with gonorrhea, can pass it on to others, and is a definite risk for future complications. Therefore, it never "hurts" to get checked for gonorrhea—it's quick, virtually painless, and confidential.

**Complications or late symptoms**/If gonorrhea is untreated, the infection spreads up the urethra and symptoms may become worse. Although, even without treatment, the symptoms can diminish and go away in about two weeks, the bacteria are still there and can cause continued destruction. The prostate gland can become infected, the testicles can become infected, and the gonococcus can spread into the bloodstream and infect various parts of the body—most commonly the joints and skin. Untreated gonorrhea can cause scarring in the urethra, in the testicles, and in the vas deferens (the tube that carries sperm from the testicles).

All of the complications of gonorrhea can be prevented by appropriate antibiotic treatment.

**Diagnosis and treatment**/The diagnosis of gonorrhea is made by examination and analysis of the penile discharge. The gonococcus bacteria are looked for under a microscope and "cultured"; that is, the discharge is placed upon culture plates containing growth media. After twenty-four hours, the plates are examined to see whether colonies of gonococci have grown on the medium. The diagnosis is easy to perform, painless, and quick.

Treatment consists of antibiotics—which may be administered as pills or by injection. One proper dose of antibiotics almost always works and kills off the gonococcus.

### *Gonorrhea in the female*

**Early symptoms**/Most women who are infected with gonorrhea do not notice any symptoms. The gonorrheal infection may begin in the cervix, which lies high and deep in the vaginal canal, so the discharge may not be noticeable. In this regard, women are much less fortunate than men, who usually have a very noticeable discharge of pus and pain upon urination. For this reason, women who have intercourse, even if they are symptom-free, should have regular cultures for gonorrhea.

Some women who are infected may notice a green or yellowish-green discharge which is usually irritating to the external genital area, the vulva. This should not be confused with one's normal vaginal discharge, which is clear or whitish and nonirritating. If the area around the urethra is infected, there may be burning upon urination. Not all vaginal discharges are caused by gonorrhea, but all discharges should be evaluated by a physician and their cause determined.

**Complications**/If a woman has no symptoms and is untreated for the infection, the gonococcus may ascend and infect her uterus. This usually occurs during menstruation, when the gonococcus can more easily enter her uterus and fallopian tubes. Pus can form within the tubes and can leak out around the ovaries and into the pelvis. This is called pelvic inflammatory disease (PID). The woman will usually develop severe lower abdominal pains, have a fever, and feel quite ill. The pain can be severe enough to mimic appendicitis.

Untreated PID can cause death. The treatment consists of antibiotics and is quite successful in killing off the gonococcus bacteria; the infection in the fallopian tubes, however, can cause significant scarring, enough to block the tubes so that the ova cannot travel from the ovaries to the uterus. Thus, gonococcal infection of the fallopian tubes is a leading cause of infertility.

In addition, if the gonococcus gets into the bloodstream, the infection can spread throughout the body. The joints and skin are primary sites of attack. This can be a very severe and life-threatening infection.

If a pregnant woman has gonorrhea, the newborn baby can catch it during the birth process as he passes through the vaginal canal. This is why penicillin ointment or silver nitrate solution is placed in the eyes of newborns—to prevent them from getting gonorrheal eye infections if their mothers have unsuspected and untreated infection.

**Diagnosis and treatment**/The only way to diagnose gonorrhea in a woman is to culture the vagina (and frequently the anus as well.) There are no blood tests that can diagnose gonorrhea. Obtaining a culture is painless, easy to do, and quick. Results from the culture are usually available in one or two days.

Treatment is with the proper dose of antibiotics, either

by pills or by injection. One dose usually kills off the infecting gonococcus.

## Syphilis

Syphilis is caused by a microscopic organism, *Treponema pallidum,* which is called a spirochete because of its spiral shape. Syphilis is as old as man; prehistoric human bones have been found that bear the scars of a syphilislike disease. Although today gonorrhea is more common than syphilis, syphilis is still very much with us and is still a *very* dangerous disease. Syphilis is a complex and destructive disease which can affect each and every organ in the body. It progresses through various stages: In the early stages it is easily treatable and can be cured; in the late stages it may be impossible to stop its progression. *Syphilis can kill.*

**Primary syphilis**/About two weeks (it can be as long as three months) after sexual contact with an infected person, the primary sore of syphilis, the chancre, appears at the spot where syphilis entered the body. In males, it usually occurs at the tip of the penis; in females, the vaginal wall, cervix, or vulva. Therefore, in women, the chancre may not be visible. The chancre is a *painless,* hard, dull-red, open sore which may be covered with a scab, and surrounding lymph nodes may be enlarged yet *painless.* If left untreated, the chancre heals by itself in one to five weeks. The chancre is loaded with the infecting treponemata, and sexual contact will pass it on. If antibiotics are administered at this stage, the spirochetes will be killed. If left untreated, although the chancre will heal, the treponemata can enter the bloodstream and the infection can continue, even though the sore has disappeared.

**Secondary syphilis**/If primary syphilis remains untreated, the disease can progress. About four to six weeks later (maybe up to six months later), a rash usually develops. The appearance of the rash is quite variable, but the rash *does not itch or hurt*. It appears all over the body, even on the palms and soles. The rash contains millions of treponemata and is *very* contagious. The person feels quite uncomfortable and sick.

Antibiotic treatment can cure the disease even at this stage, and the person will not suffer permanent damage. If the secondary stage is left untreated, the rash will eventually disappear; this does not mean, however, that the person is cured. The treponemata continue to live.

**Latent syphilis**/Untreated secondary syphilis progresses to latent syphilis, a stage in which the person may have no symptoms for many years. About one third of these people develop late or tertiary syphilis.

**Tertiary syphilis**/There are three major types of late syphilis:

*Gummas* are large, destructive ulcers which may affect the skin, eyes, liver, lungs, muscles, and other organs. When present in the skin, they are very disfiguring. Through their growth they can destroy any organ in which they are present.

*Cardiovascular problems:* The heart and major blood vessels are affected and the infection can lead to inflammation and death.

*Neurosyphilis:* When the brain and spinal cord are affected, insanity and paralysis can result. Neurosyphilis can cause death.

**Effects on pregnant women and their babies**/If a pregnant woman gets syphilis, she can pass it to her unborn child. Syphilis can devastate the fetus and cause miscarriages and stillbirths. If the fetus survives, the newborn can be ravaged by the disease, with resultant retardation, blindness, deafness, and major skin and bony deformities. Congenital syphilis is a dreadful and life-threatening disease for the newborn.

**Diagnosis**/If a chancre sore is present, the fluid can be examined under a special kind of microscope by someone who is specially trained to identify the treponemata. In addition, there are a number of excellent blood tests to diagnose syphilis. The VDRL (which stands for Veneral Disease Research Laboratory, where it was developed) is the most commonly used blood test. It tests for antibodies that the body develops to fight the treponemata. The VDRL is the test usually obtained for marriage licenses, during pregnancy, and as part of a general checkup.

Since the primary chancre is painless, and in women it may not be visible (if it's in the vagina), any woman who is having sex should be checked regularly for syphilis. Unlike gonorrhea, there is no way at present to culture for syphilis; blood tests or special microscopic examinations of chancre fluid are still necessary.

**Treatment**/Treatment by appropriate doses of antibiotics can cure primary, secondary, and latent syphilis.

### Trichomonas Infection—"Trich"

Trichomonads are microscopic single-celled organisms which can infect the vagina or male urethra. Although the transmission of trichomonas is primarily via sexual contact, it can be acquired by coming into close contact with personal items (toilet seat, towel, washcloth, etc.) recently used by an infected person.

**Symptoms**/In the *male*, there may be no symptoms, or there may be a penile discharge. Trichomoniasis in the male is usually confined to the genitals, and complications are rare.

In the *female*, there may be an irritating, foul-smelling, and profuse vaginal discharge. The vulva and vagina can become quite itchy and reddened. There may be considerable burning pain of the vulva.

**Diagnosis**/The vaginal or penile secretion should be examined under a microscope, where the trichomonads are easily seen and identified. Microscopic examination is the only way to diagnose the infection—there are no blood tests or culture assays available as yet.

**Treatment**/Drugs are available for treating "trich." Most trichomonas infections (90 to 95 percent) can be cured by a single course of medication. However, it is imperative that *both* partners be treated at the same time. For example, if a woman is treated and her partner is not, he can reinfect her as soon as she stops taking the medication. For women, vaginal suppositories are available which, although not as effective as the pills, may be used in special situations (for example, if the woman is pregnant or is breast-feeding).

## Herpes Genitalis

Herpes genitalis is caused by the virus *Herpes simplex*. It is frequently transmitted by sexual contact, but nonsexual transmission (just "catching it") can occur.

**Symptoms**/Small, *painful* blisters can appear on the penis, vulva, vagina, or cervix. These blisters can burst and leave open, reddish sores. After a few days, the herpes sores tend to heal by themselves. However, the virus may remain and reinfect the person in the future.

**Complications/**

*Recurrent infections:* The virus may continue to reinfect the person intermittently, time and time again. Each infection is followed by a "healing" process, but the virus remains, ready to attack at the next opportunity.

*Cervical cancer:* There seems to be a relationship between repeated herpes infections and a higher incidence of cervical cancer. Therefore, in a woman who has herpes, a "Pap" test should be repeated regularly in order to detect *early* cervical cancer, which is highly curable.

*Newborn infection:* At birth, if a newborn passes through a vagina that is infected with herpes virus, the newborn can "catch" the virus. Herpes virus infection of the newborn is frequently a severe disease and often can lead to death. Therefore, cesarean section is usually performed on a pregnant woman who has herpes, so that the infant will not be exposed to the virus by passing through the infected birth canal.

**Diagnosis**/Secretions from the sore are obtained, stained with the "Pap" smear technique, and examined under a microscope. In addition, the virus may be cultured to aid in the diagnosis.

**Treatment**/There is no medication as yet available that can cure the infection. Various techniques (drugs, X ray, chemicals) have been tried, but it is very difficult to completely cure herpes virus infection.

## Pubic Lice ("Crabs")

"Crabs" are really tiny lice—a very small (pinhead-sized) louse which lives mostly in the pubic hairs. These lice can be acquired either by direct close physical contact or by sleeping in a bed that is infested by the little creatures. They can be seen with the naked eye.

**Symptoms**/Itching, due to lice bites, is the most frequent symptom. Some people may not have any symptoms. No serious complications have been reported that are caused by the lice.

**Diagnosis**/Seeing them!

**Treatment**/The lice are rapidly killed by application of the drug gamma benzene hexachloride (available under the trade name of Kwell, which comes in a lotion, cream, or shampoo). Soap and water don't help. Rapid relief can be expected from Kwell. Clothing and bed linens used in the past twenty-four hours should be thoroughly cleaned.

## Yeast Vaginitis

Although not a venereal disease, candida albicans (also called monilia or yeast) vaginitis is a frequent cause of vaginal infection. The fungus is present in many women, and exactly why it causes infection is not understood completely. Women who are diabetic, taking tetracyclines, pregnant, on birth control pills, or under emotional or physical stress are more susceptible to candida vaginitis.

**Symptoms**/Itching is a common symptom. The vagina may become bright red and tender. A thick, whitish, and curdy vaginal discharge may be present.

**Diagnosis**/Microscopic examination of the vaginal discharge reveals the yeast. Culture methods are available to confirm the diagnosis, by smearing the vaginal secretions on a special growth medium and awaiting visible growth of the yeast.

**Treatment**/Nystatin effectively controls the infection. It can be given by vaginal suppositories or vaginal cream. If symptoms persist, oral tablets of nystatin can be taken.

## Hemophilus Vaginitis

Hemophilus vaginitis has been identified only recently as a sexually transmitted disease. It is characterized by a profuse, grayish vaginal discharge which is most often quite malodorous. Usually there is little itching or irritation of the vulva and vagina, and pain with urination is uncommon. Infection is localized in the vaginal area and does not spread throughout the body.

**Diagnosis**/The bacteria can be identified by microscopic examination of vaginal secretions and confirmed by growth on culture medium.

**Treatment**/Oral antibiotics or vaginal tablets or creams containing antibiotics may be used. Since hemophilus vaginitis is transmitted through sexual contact, both partners must be treated.

# 7

# Headaches, Stomachaches, and "I Don't Feel Good"

A cut finger you can see. A bump you can feel. Fever is fever. A runny nose drips. A sore throat is red. Diarrhea is diarrhea. But "my head aches"? "my stomach hurts"? Or "I don't feel good"? How do you as a parent judge the seriousness of such subjective complaints of discomfort by your adolescent son or daughter? . . .

You can't. You have to rely on your child to tell you how much, how little, how frequently, where, and even *when* it "feels bad." Headaches and stomachaches *do* hurt—they hurt whether their cause is physical or emotional. Psychosomatic symptoms often "hurt" parents as well, for we do feel for our children. When they complain of headaches or stomachaches, we often think of headaches or stomachaches we've had and how painful they were. We thus tend to respond to our own perceptions of how our child feels. In addition, a stomachache may cause a parent to worry about appendicitis or an ulcer; headaches may bring fear of a brain tumor or some other terrible problem. For a cold or runny nose a parent may not take a child to a physician, but the fears evoked by headaches or stomachaches may certainly lead to the doctor's office.

Stomachaches or headaches, however, especially those of a long-standing or recurrent nature, are most often caused by underlying emotional difficulties—reactions to stress in the adolescent's life. Such symptoms are then called psychosomatic—physical pain that is caused by mental pain. The psychosomatic complaint is a *symptom,* not of underlying physical problems, but of underlying emotional problems—most often anxiety, adjustment difficulties, anger, sadness, or depression.

It is helpful to view psychosomatic complaints as a plea for emotional help, a request that the adolescent cannot express through words but can express through bodily complaints. Although these complaints are cries for *emotional* help, all too frequently only *physical* help is given. If we focus on the physical symptoms and the bodily pain, we often overlook the underlying emotional struggles that are generating the pain.

Adolescents who have psychosomatic complaints usually have parents who find it easier to accept and to act upon physical complaints than emotional ones. Many parents tend to pay much more attention to, and be more sympathetic toward, physical complaints than emotional ones. *Psychosomia, therefore, is a two-way street between parent and teenager.* The teenager who feels emotional conflict, but who doesn't feel comfortable in expressing his troubles verbally, uses a headache or a stomachache to get his parents' attention. When parents do pay attention to the physical or somatic complaint, this is reassuring to the adolescent; the underlying psychological issues, however, remain unfaced and unresolved. It is no wonder, then, that such physical complaints tend to recur and recur.

*Why would an adolescent "choose" to suffer psychosomatic symptoms rather than to express his feelings directly?*
An adolescent doesn't consciously think, "Well, should I talk about what's bothering me, or should I just get sick?" Once again, we should recognize that adolescence is not the beginning of a teenager's life; emotional responses and behavior learned during childhood will dominate the adolescent's thinking and reactions. If a child learns that a good way to get parental attention is to be physically sick but that a good way to evoke parental anger or indifference is to verbalize emotional feelings, he will probably become physically sick when he needs parental attention. Unfortunately, the same parents who attend to physical illness with great compassion often respond to emotional problems with indifference. In general, parents tend to respond to their children in much the same way their parents responded to them.

I want to reemphasize that the adolescent's learned responses to emotional conflicts develop as a result of childhood experiences and are quite subliminal; that is, they do not represent conscious thinking. *Psychosomatic illness is not deliberate.* We should not become angry at adolescents who have psychosomatic complaints, nor should we dismiss them as "little bellyachers" or "crybabies." We should realize that the complaint is a plea for parenting or emotional help—a plea expressed through bodily discomfort.

If we respond only to our adolescent's behavior (in this case, psychosomatic complaints) and not to the underlying feelings from which the behavior evolved, we may become angry at our teenager. When a child continually complains of "hurting" and we can offer nothing that helps, we may become frustrated by our inability to provide relief or comfort. Such frustrations may lead us to feel guilty about our inability to care properly for our child and, ultimately, to feel anger toward the child for making us feel guilty. As long as we focus on the symptom instead of on the underlying feeling, the symptom will continue to recur and we may become angrier and angrier—which is exactly the opposite of the response our adolescent wants and needs. Inevitably, everybody pays a price for not being direct and not expressing feelings openly.

*Why did the adolescent "choose" a particular symptom?*
Psychosomatic illness is a family disease.

Statistically, parents of children with recurrent abdominal pain are six times more likely to have had abdominal pain themselves than are parents of children without recurrent abdominal pain. Adolescents with recurrent stomachaches, therefore, frequently have a parent after whom they have "modeled" their psychosomatic complaints. Parents who are "somatizers" (express feelings primarily through "body talk" rather than verbally) should not be too surprised when their children pick up and learn such traits and become "somatizers" themselves.

When an adolescent complains of stomachaches, headaches, or "I don't feel good," he is often reflecting his family's way of responding to emotional conflict; *his* pattern of reaction through pyschosomia parallels a similar *family* pattern. In addition, adolescents don't just pick a symptom out of the blue; the symptom is modeled after another person's symptom—somebody the adolescent knows (most often, another family member), has read about, or has seen on television or in the movies.

The adolescent, therefore, tends to "model" his psychosomatic behaviors after: (1) his family's pattern of psychosomatic response to stress and/or (2) a particular person with a similar type of complaint. The following case histories illustrate "modeling" behavior:

Bobbie, fifteen, had headaches for years. She had neither sinus troubles nor brain tumors, but she did have a mother who had recurrent headaches which increased when her husband left on business trips, headaches so severe that she had to remain in bed and have Bobbie take care of her.

When tensions arose in Bobbie's own life, Bobbie would get headaches and Mother would "care" for her. "Poor darling, I know just how she feels." Mother would sympathize. With counseling, Bobbie recognized that her headaches enabled her to avoid facing difficulties and also got Mother to take care of her. The difficulties wouldn't go away, however, nor would her headaches. Only later, as Bobbie became more comfortable in her ability to face life's problems, did the frequency and intensity of her headaches decrease. In addition, Bobbie came to realize how angry and manipulated she felt by her mother's headaches. When Mother complained of headaches and dashed for the bed, Bobbie felt less and less need to take care of her. Initially, Mother was hurt at Bobbie's "heartless" response and frequently sighed, "after all I've done for her!" Subsequently, however, Mother was able to realize how anxious she felt when her husband was away, and she began to work out these feelings directly with her husband.

Ronald, a small, thin boy of fourteen, had stomachaches

before gym class. His visits to the school nurse were nearly equal in number to his scheduled visits to the gym. His father had a peptic ulcer which often kept him home from work at a job he hated. Ronald, feeling himself to be a "weakling," was extremely embarrassed about the communal showers that followed gym class. In much the same way his father did, Ronald "used" stomachaches to avoid doing something he didn't want to do.

Sid's parents both worked long, hard hours in the family store. Come rain, come shine, they went to work. Sid came into my office complaining that he was "so tired all the time." He couldn't keep up with his eighth-grade schoolwork. His "no-nonsense" parents didn't talk of feelings, of emotions. They were good people who simply were not at all psychologically oriented. When I talked with Sid, he remembered that four years before, his mother had taken time off from work when her mother was suffering from cancer and needed her help. Sid didn't believe he had cancer, but he did remember how *tired* his grandmother had been . . . and that his mother took care of her. Sid, subconsciously, was trying to get his mother to care for him as she had done for his grandmother.

Another case was Derek, aged sixteen, who complained of severe pains in his hands. One year earlier Derek had had a mild arthritis, probably viral in origin, which would have cleared up on its own except that a physician mistakenly mentioned that it might have been rheumatoid arthritis. Derek didn't know what rheumatoid arthritis was and wasn't too concerned until he unfortunately saw a television show in which a young boy was crippled and wheelchair-bound from rheumatoid arthritis. Derek was overwhelmed and convinced that the same fate would shortly befall him. He modeled his behavior, not after a family member or acquaintance, but after a character in a television show. It took months for Derek to accept the fact that he didn't have rheumatoid arthritis and that he was indeed healthy.

*What precipitated the psychosomatic symptom?*
Although psychosomatic symptoms usually represent learned behavioral responses to stress, frequently a precipitating factor evokes or triggers the psychosomatic response. Such a factor may be a sudden emotional upset or traumatic event. It is often helpful to consider, "Why now?" What has caused the adolescent to have the symptom? What's going on in the adolescent's life that may have triggered the psychosomatic behavior?

No matter what the specific precipitating event, the most frequent underlying emotional stress preceding psychosomatic symptoms is the *fear of losing something* without having an adequate substitute to replace the loss. The loss may be real, threatened, or imagined, and although it usually relates to a loss of a family member or close friend, it may also be caused by a fear of loss or decline of physical or intellectual capabilities, school grades, job, reputation, or just the adolescent's previous sense of well-being. Coincidental with the actual, threatened, or imagined loss is a continuing, unrelieved, and overwhelming frustration in coping with the feelings and an inability to deal comfortably with the impact of the loss. The precipitating factor, therefore, may be real or fantasized and may be derived from a wide range of sources. The vast majority of these factors have their sources in home, school, or peer group experiences.

*Home.* The adolescent may fear that someone in the family may die or that family discord will lead to separation or divorce. Or these events may have taken place. The adolescent may be identifying with someone in the family who is sick, or may be caught up in parental preoccupation with illness—"familial hypochondriasis." On occasion, adolescents may be having difficulty in handling pent-up angry feelings about parents or may have unsatisfying relationships with their parents.

Perhaps the most frequent precipitating factor is that the

parents are having difficulties in getting along with one another and the adolescent is caught up in their struggles. (See Chapter 9 concerning the impact of divorce on the adolescent.)

*School.* School is the major "work" of the adolescent. Many of the problems that adolescents have in school closely parallel the kinds of difficulties adults have at work. A particular teacher (supervisor), a particular subject (work task), an examination (quality controls), school grades (evaluations), other kids in the classroom (co-workers), what courses to take (decisions), homework (overtime), change from one school to another (job change)—either singly or all together—can precipitate psychosomatic illness. I might add that writing a theme paper (writing a book) can fit in there as well!

*Peers.* I'm so glad we only have to go through adolescence once. Few of us would have the energy to survive the fears, anxieties, frustrations, disappointments, and pimples once again; many of us still get headaches, stomachaches, and "don't feel good" just reminiscing about it. Specific precipitating factors which can evoke psychosomatic illness include dating, drugs, sex, acceptance by peers, driving, and sports, to name a few. When psychosomatic behavior is triggered by peer experiences, the adolescent often has an underlying fear of losing the acceptance or approval of his peers.

*What gains does the adolescent derive from the psychosomatic behavior?*

Any behavior engaged in over a period of time, even seemingly unpleasant behavior, must be providing some degree of gain or satisfaction; otherwise, the behavior would most likely cease. If we are to understand psychosomatic behavior, it is important to identify what the adolescent gains from hurting. Gain accrues when the psychosomatic behavior enables the adolescent to *avoid* or *control* a situation. For example, stomachaches may keep the adolescent from going to school; headaches may avoid chores; and "being sick" may tend to keep parents from fighting (control them). Gains also occur when the behavior results in the adolescent receiving more *attention* and/or *emotional caretaking* from parents, other family members, or friends. Unfortunately, such attention does not always help the adolescent deal with the problems underlying the psychosomatic behavior. Although gains may result that *temporarily* ease or soothe the underlying emotional pain, they do not serve to help resolve the underlying problems. That's one reason why psychosomatic behavior recurs: Until the generating emotional conflict is resolved, the physical pains will resurface again and again.

Another reason for the persistence of psychosomia is that a secondary gain may become important to the adolescent. For example, Sid, the boy discussed previously whose parents worked long hours in the store, acted tired all the time and thereby gained Mother's attention and caretaking. His underlying feeling was that his mother didn't love him; otherwise, why would she work such long hours? Originally, the primary gain of his psychosomatic behavior was to control the amount of time his mother worked; secondarily, he gained his mother's attention. In time, his mother's attention became the dominant gain, and Sid persisted in "being tired all the time." Still unresolved was his conflict over whether his mother loved him. He had manipulated her into taking care of him, yet he still was not certain whether she loved him. If, at the *inception* of Sid's psychosomatic behavior, his parents or others had recognized that something was bothering him emotionally and helped him to identify and work through the problem, both Sid and his parents would have been saved a great deal of heartache. With assistance, Sid was able to understand his mother's love for him and reconcile it with her desire to work for the welfare of the entire family.

Sid began to work with his parents in the family store, and his fatigability subsided.

Gains from psychosomatic behavior are illustrated in the following cases:

Jill, aged twelve, had such severe stomachaches that she frequently missed school. When she stayed at home, her mother would also stay home from work.

*Gain:* Stay home from school, and have Mother stay home with her.
*Underlying problem:* Jill hated to come home to an empty house after school. When Jill began to participate in extracurricular activities, spending time with her friends after school and returning home only after her mother or dad had arrived, her stomachaches subsided. Jill still feels somewhat angry about having a working mother but now is able to express these feelings verbally.

David, aged fifteen, had stomachaches of such frequency and severity that he often missed school. When David stayed home, he had to stay in his room and do homework.

*Gain:* Stay home from school, have parents know he is home.
*Underlying problem:* David's father had a drinking problem and sometimes would beat his wife during the day. When his father was drinking, David was afraid to leave his mother at home alone; he felt that he had to protect her from his father. When his father went into counseling, stopped drinking, and stopped attacking his mother, David could comfortably return to school. He no longer needed to have stomachaches.

Jonathan's abdominal pains were so severe that they doubled him over. His parents were constantly fighting and contemplating divorce. Whenever Jonathan had these pain attacks, his parents would rush him to the doctor's office—and would stay there with him, together. They were genuinely concerned about Jonathan, so concerned that they would stop fighting when he had an attack.

> *Gain:* Keep parents from fighting, attention from parents.
> *Underlying problem:* Jonathan was afraid he would lose his father if his parents divorced. When Jonathan became able to discuss with his parents his concerns over the divorce, he no longer had to resort to psychosomatic behavior.

Bill, twelve, was angry at his parents because they spent most evenings away from home. He didn't want a baby-sitter—he wanted his parents. Bill developed "seizures"—a condition that "freaked out" all available baby-sitters and thus curtailed his parents' social life.

> *Gain:* Parents at home.
> *Underlying problem:* Bill was unable to verbalize his anger at his parents for not spending time with him. He never complained when they went out; his parents didn't know he cared. His "seizures" served to keep them at home, though they were angry at Bill for being a burden. During family therapy, Bill gradually became able to verbalize his feelings and no longer had to rely upon his psychosomatic behavior to express them.

Shirley had begun to have headaches and feel tired most of the time. She just had no energy to do anything except her schoolwork, at which she excelled. Her father had lost his job and was depressed. Her mother cried all the time. They couldn't talk with her or with each other about how they were feeling, so they just moped around the house. Together they brought Shirley to the office. When I saw Shirley, she felt fine, but she was quite concerned about her parents.

> *Gain:* Control of the situation, in getting parents to bring her to the office.
> *Underlying problem:* Concern over her parents' health. After interviewing Shirley's parents, it was quite obvious that they

were having serious emotional problems; a social worker is now seeing them in therapy. Shirley is fine. She had used psychosomatic complaints to bring her parents into a setting where they could receive help with their problems.

This case illustrates that almost invariably, when an adolescent shows psychosomatic behavior, *parents need help as much as the adolescent does.*

*How can parents manage a teenager who shows psychosomatic behavior?*
1. Try to establish why the psychosomatic behavior is taking place.
Since psychosomatic behavior is often a response to underlying emotional stress and is a *plea for help,* it is helpful to determine what precipitating factors may have triggered the behavior. Exploring with your adolescent how things are going at home, at school, and within his peer group will usually shed light on what's troubling him.

2. Recognize that adolescents usually model their symptoms after someone who has a similar symptom.
If you can determine after whom the adolescent has modeled his behavior, this can illuminate both the underlying problem and what the adolescent hopes to gain from his behavior. Adolescents tend to model after someone whose psychosomatic behavior has, in their eyes, "paid off" in a way that they would like theirs to do.

3. Determine what gains are derived from the behavior.
Although difficult for a parent to do, it is important to look at your adolescent objectively and ask yourself, "What is he gaining by hurting?" This is painful, for often we have helped to perpetuate the behavior by allowing gain to take place. After defining the gain, we can then take measures to

decrease it while searching for the underlying problem which generated the behavior.

4. Don't focus on the physical aspects of psychosomatic complaints.

If your adolescent is reluctant to communicate with you verbally and, at the moment, can do so only through physical pain, let him know that you realize he is in pain, but don't focus on the physical aspects of the complaint. Instead, encourage him to talk about any precipitating events and underlying emotional problems. Don't be surprised if efforts to take care of the physical problem don't work. Aspirin won't make psychosomatic headaches disappear; antacids won't stop psychosomatic stomachaches; and vitamins won't relieve psychosomatic "I don't feel good." What adolescents want and need from us is parenting and love, not pills and drugs.

5. Don't get angry.

Pain *is* pain, regardless of cause, and your adolescent is *not* being sick "on purpose." Though there is a "purpose" for the psychosomatic behavior, an adolescent is usually unaware of the connection between his unresolved problems and his illness. Awareness of the connection will not necessarily "cure" the pain; the underlying problems need to be resolved.

6. Recognize that psychosomia is usually a family affair.

Many families have at least one adult whose reaction to stress takes the form of physical symptoms. When parents or other family members display psychosomatic behaviors, it's no wonder that children pick up these maladaptive ways of coping and use them in an attempt to solve their own problems.

7. Remember, psychosomatic behavior is a plea for help.

Our "little bellyachers" are trying to tell us something. We may not want to hear what they are going to say, because it often involves a request for us to change our own behavior, but we must listen to them.

If parents respond to psychosomatic behavior by helping their adolescents define and work through underlying emotional problems, the pain of psychosomia will have served a useful purpose.

# 10

# Famous One-Liners

Many adolescents and parents use common phrases, or "one-liners," to express their feelings. Why do they say these things? What do they really mean? What unspoken, yet implied, messages do these one-liners convey? What are the underlying anxieties, fears, concerns, and expectations that these phrases express? Let's analyze some of these famous one-liners, beginning with those that adolescents are likely to hurl. . . .

# I. ADOLESCENT TO PARENT

**"All You Care About Is Money!"**/This one-liner can have a devastating effect on parents. How could their teenager have possibly reached this conclusion? How could he so misunderstand their values and motives?

To a degree, parents create this problem when they attempt to control their children and adolescents through money: "If you do this chore, I'll pay you for it." "If you're *good*, I'll buy you a present." "If you're *bad*, you won't get your allowance." When parents place a price tag on their adolescent's behavior, they reveal the importance they place upon money.

When a mother works outside the home, or when a father is preoccupied with business concerns and spends little time with his family, a child may conclude that money is more important to his parents than he is. Also, parents may confuse their children inadvertently when they say, "We work hard to earn money because we love you." An adolescent may have learned to equate love with money and to believe: "If my parents give me money, they are giving me love; if they withhold money, they are withholding love."

Another way to interpret this one-liner is with the realization that most adolescents don't have much money, usually cannot earn very much, and are largely dependent upon their parents for money; therefore, they may be somewhat jealous of their parents, who do have money. Many things that adolescents want cost a significant amount of money: cars, clothes, stereos, sports equipment, musical instruments, etc. Often, parents seem like the "haves" and adolescents feel like the "have-nots." When a "have" parent says no to a "have-not" adolescent, the teenager's anger may emerge as "All you care about is money"—which implies "and not about me."

An adolescent may deny the importance of money because a need for money may imply dependence upon parents, a state from which he is struggling to free himself. It's
difficult for an adolescent to think of himself as independent
when he frequently has to ask his parents for money. It is
therefore important to encourage your teenager to earn
money, both to decrease his dependence upon you and to
increase his self-confidence through the realization that he
can provide for some of his own monetary needs.

Many adolescents are very idealistic about fairness and
equality and have a romantic concept of the way people
should relate and share with one another. Many adolescents
are more people-oriented than money-oriented and may
question the materialistic values held by their parents.
Although a part of the teenager's rejection of parental
materialistic values may be considered as a normal adolescent process, an element of such rejection may be the
adolescent's genuine wish for the world to be more fair and
just.

If our adolescents accuse us of caring only about money,
we should not try to squelch them with such retorts as, "If
you feel that way, I won't give you any money" or "Try living
without it." If we respond to their questioning of our material values by threatening to control them through money,
we just reinforce their belief that all we care about is money.
Perhaps a better way to respond would be by saying, "Money
*is* important—we all need it to live. But people are also
important. Caring about money doesn't mean that you can't
care about people."

**"Stop Treating Me Like a Baby!"**/Most of us have heard
parents say: "I can't believe that he is already a teenager!" "I
can't be old enough to have an adolescent." Or, "You'll
always be my baby." Parents tend to view their children as
younger than they really are. It's hard for many parents to

admit that their darling, sweet child is now an adolescent. This means that the parents are older as well.

Some parents have difficulty in transferring some of the decision-making responsibilities to their adolescents. With younger children, parents have to make almost all decisions for their child—the child's very safety may be at stake. But to promote the development of adolescents, parents must permit them to make many decisions on their own. When an adolescent protests, "Stop treating me like a baby," he is also saying, "I can do it by myself ... I can make up my own mind."

To stop treating an adolescent as a baby means that parents have to loosen, not cut, the proverbial apron strings and let the adolescent become more independent in his decisions. Allowing the adolescent to make his own decisions is often quite difficult, especially when we think our teenager is making a poor choice. If that choice does not place him in jeopardy, parents should go along with the decision and let him find out on his own the consequences of his decision, learn from his own experience. If he regrets his decision, parents should refrain from saying, "I told you so," which implies that you are wise and he is not. Such a statement will only make him angry and cause him to lose confidence in his ability to make decisions. If you must say something when it's obvious that he has made an error in judgment, it's much more beneficial to say "Part of growing up is learning from your own decisions."

Parents should stop treating their adolescent "like a baby," yet they should not treat him as an adult; he is still dependent upon them for many things. Parents often feel that they are balancing on a seesaw: Are they giving too much responsibility? Too little? Or just enough? And what is enough? These are difficult questions because each adolescent is unique in the amount of responsibility he can accept comfortably. Parents must decide how much responsibility is best for their adolescent.

**"You Don't Understand *Anything!*"**/Parents may congratulate themselves when their adolescent says to them, "You don't understand *anything!*" This one-liner may indicate that you are successful parents—your child is now acting like a normal adolescent. Deprecation of parents and partial rejection of parental ideas and values are typical processes that the adolescent uses to achieve emotional separation. Your adolescent must have established a degree of self-identity and self-esteem in order to utter this one-liner. He is saying that he disagrees with you, thereby implying that he has his own ideas and insights which he thinks are more appropriate than yours. Many adolescents need to "put down" their parents in order to justify moving away from them emotionally. If parents were seen as perfect, it would be much more difficult for the adolescent to consider his differing ideas as important; thus his emotional development would be hampered. As your adolescent matures further, he will become more selective about the areas in which he disagrees with you; the younger adolescent is much more likely to generalize and say that you don't understand *anything*. Rather than interpret his "You don't understand anything" as disrespectful, parents can instead appreciate this one-liner as a signal that their adolescent is thinking for himself and beginning to stand on his own two feet.

**"I Hate School!"**/Adolescents don't have to love school. If your teenager announces "I hate school," he may be having a normal adolescent reaction to school's rules and regulations or to teachers who tell him what to do. Or he may be having problems with school grades, classmates, or teachers. If there are problems at home, he may claim to hate school so that he can stay home to keep an eye on what's going on there (for example, his parents may be fighting, or a family member may be ill).

The key point, once again, is that we should focus on what our adolescent is trying to communicate rather than upon his words. He must explore whether his "hating school" represents a temporary feeling or a difficult problem. He may be feeling pressure to achieve high grades or may be doing poorly in his schoolwork. Perhaps his classmates are picking on him, or a school bully may be after him. A personality conflict with one of his teachers may be interfering with his studies. In such instances, we should let him decide how to manage his problems. We can offer suggestions, but it is up to him to try to remedy the situation. School is his responsibility, and we should allow him the opportunity to work things out. If his efforts don't succeed, then we can intervene.

When there are problems at home, the entire family is involved and the situation may be more difficult. If parents are arguing, they should explain to their adolescent that the dissensions are between them and it is up to them to solve their problems; it's not up to him to be a mediator of their differences. If someone at home is ill, again the adolescent should be assured that it's not his job to be the caretaker during the day; his job is to be a student in school. If at all possible, teenagers should not have to miss school in order to care for a family member who is ill.

While many adolescents complain about school, label their teachers as "dumb," and feel that their courses are irrelevant, the teenager who proclaims that he hates school may be having more than his expected share of difficulties. If his problems remain unresolved, eventually he may drop out of school and thus may create even more problems for himself. We, as parents, must keep this from happening. We can do so by responding to our adolescent's concerns and helping him to solve his problems.

**"I Don't Care How It Was When You Were My Age!"**/Since most parents have learned how to parent from their own parents, they tend to treat their teenagers in much the same way they, as teenagers, were treated by their parents. "If it was good enough for me, it's good enough for you." "I had to do it, so you have to do it." If we expect our adolescents to do things just because we had to, and lose sight of the differences between their growing up and our growing up, we can expect them to protest, "I don't care how it was when you were my age." Times *are* different for them today than they were for us as teenagers (see Chapter 1). Yet many values of yesteryear retain their timeliness and appropriateness and still serve as the basis for the standards of behavior we expect of our adolescents. It's just that we should relate our values to the present time, rather than rely on repeating what our parents said to us. For example, it's more beneficial for your adolescent if you say, "I believe that if you want something, it's best for you to have to work for it" instead of "My parents never gave that to me—I had to work for it." The basic theme of earning what you want remains, but it is rephrased to show your concern for what's best for your adolescent and to indicate that the beliefs are your own, not somebody else's old beliefs.

Your adolescent will be more likely to accept and abide by your decisions if you consider him as an individual. If you find yourself wanting to say "When I was your age . . ." or some similar phrase, it's a good time to stop and reconsider the situation: Is this decision based upon what *you think best* for the adolescent at this time, or is it based upon what *your parents thought best for you* when you were a teenager? If it's the latter, your adolescent may be justified in using this one-liner.

**"You Don't Care About Me."**/Why do adolescents so often accuse their parents of not caring? What do teenagers really mean by this statement?

This one-liner is often hurled at parents who have just said no to their teenager or who have expressed anger at his behavior. The teenager might be angry about the "no" and hope that the accusation of not caring will make his parents feel guilty enough to change their answer to yes, thereby "proving" that they do care. Or sometimes a teenager may misinterpret his parent's "no" or expression of anger to mean that his parents really don't care: "If they feel that way, they must not love me." In such a case, the teenager is simply asking for reassurance that the parents do care.

At times, adolescents would *temporarily* like to believe that their parents don't care about them. Since adolescents use alienation from parents to ease the pain of emotional separation, thinking that parents "don't care" could help to validate a teenager's feelings of alienation. "If my parents don't care about me, I don't have to care about them."

Another underlying reason may be that adolescents may fantasize their parents as "perfect parents"—parents who love them so much that anything they do is okay. "Perfect parents" would forgive any wrongdoing with a mild reprimand ("Just don't do it again"). When parents legitimately become angry at their adolescent's behavior, the teenager's overreaction of "You don't care about me!" may be due to feelings that the "perfect parents" are no longer perfect.

"You don't care about me" or a similar statement, "Nobody likes me," often evokes a rapid parental response of "But of course we care for you" or "People *do* like you." When that happens, we have responded only to our adolescent's behavior; however, if we focus on the underlying feelings that led to the one-liner, we can help them define their anger or concerns. One way to respond to your adolescent is: "I do care about you—even when I say no or become angry at your behavior. Not liking what you have done doesn't mean that I don't like you. Yet I wonder what you were feeling when you said that I don't care about you."

## "How Come the Rules Are Different for *Me?*"

"How come *he* gets to stay out later than *I* do?"

"Why don't you make *her* pick up *her* things?"

"How come you always give *me* the hard jobs and give *him* the easy ones?"

"Why do you let *them* get away with everything?"

"How come you let *her* have the car whenever she wants it?"

"*He* never cleans up *his* filthy room—why do I have to keep mine clean?"

"You love her more than you love me!"

"I had to go to bed at nine when I was his age—why doesn't *he?*"

"You always let *her* do whatever she wants."

"How come *his* allowance is bigger than *mine?*"

"She's got *twice* as many clothes as I have."

"How come *he* can sleep over and *I* can't?"

"How come *I* was grounded for that and *he* wasn't?"

"You don't yell at *him* when *he* gets a D!"

Parents often do treat and discipline their children differently from one another. This could be because they recognize that their children are individuals with distinct needs and capabilities and should be regarded as different. It may be that parents actually prefer one of their children over another; or it may be that, through experience, parents have become more or less liberal in their child-rearing practices. In any circumstance, adolescents will be aware of the differences in the way their parents treat them. What an adolescent *must not* feel is that parents favor one sibling over another: This implies that one is good and the other is bad.

It's nearly impossible for parents to be completely even-handed in their approach to their adolescents. What parents can do to temper the differences is to regard each adolescent as an individual and *never, never* compare one to another.

Parental decisions should be based upon what's best for the particular adolescent, not upon what was done previously for another. This does not imply favoritism; it does recognize that each child matures and behaves differently and has different needs. Nevertheless, parents are often in a no-win situation. If parents treat all their children the same, their adolescents will protest that they are individuals and should be treated differently; if parents treat their children differently, their adolescents will protest that they should be treated the same. Parents must emphasize that they care about each one of their children, and what they let one do and don't let another do is based upon appreciation of them as individuals.

**"You Can't Make Me!"**/Of course you can, and—when so challenged by your adolescent regarding an important matter—you must. Throughout this book it has been stressed repeatedly that we, as parents, should focus primarily upon the reasons for our adolescent's behavior rather than upon the behavior itself. There are times, however, when the first thing we must do is take action, before exploring the underlying reasons: when our teenager's health or safety is involved, and when he says defiantly, "You can't make me!"

Saying "make me" is distinctly different from saying "I don't want to do it." In the latter, he is expressing his feelings and desires and is often willing to discuss the situation. In the former, he is issuing an ultimatum —the situation is often past the point of negotiation.

Often, when an adolescent says "You can't make me," subconsciously he *wants* you to tell him to do it. He is testing parental authority to determine how independent he really is. If parents then say, "Do what you want," they are abdicating their responsibility for supervising or protecting him. Another basis for the one-liner may be that the adolescent wants his parents to become angry at him. "Make me" invariably achieves that goal.

After parents have responded to the adolescent's challenge, then they can ask him what was going on that caused him to defy them so vehemently.

## II. PARENT TO ADOLESCENT

**"We'll See . . ."**/"We'll see . . ." a phrase used by parents when they want to delay making a commitment—especially when they really want to say no. Why is it so difficult for parents to say no to their adolescent?

Many parents find it easier to say no to a child than to an adolescent. Children require parental guidance in almost all matters; in many situations, their very safety may be at stake. Young children tend to accept parental decisions and rarely protest for too long. They seldom make the case that, since other children can do something, why can't they? Young children don't persist in asking parents, "Why not?" And if a child asks for something and his parents respond with "We'll see," often he'll forget about the matter and not bring it up again.

The adolescent's response to a parental "no" is quite different. Adolescents can make up their own minds about many issues and don't require parental decisions for most matters. When told no, they often will not only protest, but will also come forth with logical and well-prepared arguments. Teenagers are experts at collecting evidence to support their views: "All my friends can do it!" or "I'm the only kid in my school who has to do that!" Adolescents are guaranteed to ask, "Why not?" and will persist in arguing with your "no." And unlike a young child who may forget a request after a response of "We'll see," an adolescent displays an elephant-like memory of the request. ("They should remember their schoolwork that well!" lamented one parent.)

In addition, parents may have difficulty in saying no because their adolescent may be asking to do something that his parents themselves wanted to do, or did, when they were his age. For example, an adolescent may want to stay out until 1 A.M. when the house rules state midnight. His father may remember when *he* stayed out until one, or wanted to, and his parents said no. House rules are house rules . . . but what the heck, it's only one hour more. . . . Hence the indecision and the hedge of "We'll see." I strongly recommend that, as parents, we say no when we mean no, yes when we mean yes, and "We'll see" only when we *do* intend to see—to consider the matter thoughtfully. A good way to astonish your adolescent is to go up to him and say, "Remember when I said 'We'll see'? Well, I've thought about it, and my answer is yes [or no]." "We'll see" should mean that you are taking the request under advisement and that an answer will be forthcoming.

We should not use "We'll see" as "bribery"—that is, "If you do this [and perhaps a number of unmentioned things as well], maybe I'll do that." Such a method of managing children is neither effective nor constructive, and it's a poor method for them to learn. If you do it to them, they'll probably do it to you whenever they get the chance. Let's deal directly and honestly with our adolescents.

**"Don't Do As I Do—Do As I Say!"**/Parents often see in their children an idealized version of themselves, that part of themselves that wants to be perfect or near perfect, and look upon their children as symbols of all that is good and honest. The phrase "the innocence of children" may be interpreted to mean that children are not "corrupted" as yet by the pressures and strains of living in a complex, adult world. Many of us try to keep our children "good" through guiding words; since we are human, however, our behavior is never quite as ideal as our words. Our children are observant and aware; they watch us closely and readily perceive the differences between our words and our behavior. So when we say one thing, then behave differently, they catch us in a bind which often leads us to say, "Don't do as I do—do as I say."

For example, my daughter was in the car when I received a justifiable citation for exceeding the speed limit (just a little). I have frequently discussed with her the need to obey traffic laws. When she receives her first traffic ticket—and I become righteously indignant about it—she may remind me of *my* traffic ticket. I'll probably respond with, "Don't do as I do—do as I say." When she retorts "Gotcha!" she'll be right.

We would like to be perfect parents, but our behavior is imperfect. Our children, being human like us, will make some mistakes, usually similar to the kind we make. Yet *we often expect more of our children than we do of ourselves.* Our children are not idealized versions of ourselves; they are themselves and reflect our imperfections as well. "Don't do as I do—do as I say," although frequently the only thing parents can think of saying at the time, is an unfair thing to ask of an adolescent. "Do as I say, and I'll try to do the same" is a lot harder for parents to live up to, yet a great deal more realistic.

**"Am I Talking to Myself?"**/Adolescents just don't seem to linger on each and every insightful, meaningful, caring, and guiding word of parental wisdom. We should be thankful they don't; if they did, something would be *very* wrong.

Since for adolescents alienation from parents and the rejection or deprecation of parental values are ways to achieve emotional emancipation and to establish self-identity, parents should not be too surprised when their adolescents don't seem to listen to what they have to say. If adolescents listened to and heeded all parental advice, they would be, in essence, carbon-copy versions of their parents. They would not accomplish self-development.

Adolescents want to be independent of their parents, while at the same time they are—and need to be—dependent upon them. So adolescents have some conflicting feelings when parents tell them what to do. They want the advice; they don't want to listen.

Parental advice usually falls upon a stonelike face and "deaf"ears, but the adolescent *does* hear what is being said. If the adolescent agrees with what his parents are saying, he tends to remain acceptingly quiet; but, behold!, if the adolescent disagrees with what his parents are saying, his blank expression changes at once into an animated caricature of an outraged adolescent. Many parents would immediately faint if their adolescent said, "Gee, Mom, that sounds terrific ... thanks a lot." Knowing that their adolescents are unlikely to respond verbally to advice, parents often gently coerce them with such loving words as, "Just grunt, so I'll know you heard me."

It is frustrating when your teenager doesn't acknowledge that he has heard what you have said. Yet *actions speak louder than words*. Usually, your adolescent's behavior will signal that he has listened. When parents realize that a stoic response from a teenager is normal and to be expected, they can stop asking, "Am I talking to myself?"

**"I Can't Stand Those Kids You Hang Around With!"**/Yes, your adolescent's friends probably do look and act different from the kinds of friends you wish he had. They may be rude, unkempt, inconsiderate, unmotivated, and deliberately irritating. It may be all you can do to be civil to them. Yet your teenager needs his friends, and they need him; they need each other to be "different" with.

Sometimes it's easier for parents to see "faults," qualities they don't approve of, in their adolescent's friends than it is for them to see similar qualities in their own teenager. For many parents, it's easier to focus on the behavior of someone else's adolescent than upon the behavior of their own. For the most part, the characteristics that parents like or dislike in their adolescent's friends are found in their own teenager as well. If you don't like your adolescent's friends, it may help to keep in mind the importance of the peer group in providing an arena for behavioral experimentation and a set of standards (different from yours) to which your teenager can conform while achieving his emotional separation from you and seeking his own identity. When parents recognize the value of the peer group for their adolescent, much of his peer-oriented behavior will make more sense and even his friends may become more acceptable.

**"I Don't Care If Your Friends Can ... You Can't!"**/In today's highly mobile and transient society, few traditional ethnic neighborhoods still exist. One advantage of a homogeneous ethnic neighborhood is that most families share similar moral beliefs. The unwritten moral code, which is set by community standards, dictates expected behaviors—of both parents and teenagers. In heterogeneous neighborhoods, there is often an admixture of various moral beliefs—some strict, some lenient. When parents in the community don't agree themselves on the expected standards for adolescent behavior, the adolescent may be confused by the differing attitudes and rules. Bewildered teenagers may ask, "Everybody else can, why can't I?" Certainly parents don't have to let their teenagers do something simply because other parents let their teenagers do it. Within reason, parents are entitled to raise their children as they think best, even when their beliefs differ from those of other parents in the community.

Subconsciously, your adolescent often likes you to tell him what to do. It shows that you care enough about him to tell him what to do and to give guidance based upon what you believe to be correct. If you didn't care about him, what he did would be of minor concern to you. A laissez-faire attitude may imply an "I don't care" attitude. When you tell him what to do, or say no, he may grumble and complain, but at the same time he'll realize that you do stick up for what you believe. If your decision is at variance with his peers' parents' decisions, share with your adolescent the rationale of your decision, acknowledge that it's different from that of his friends' parents, and reiterate that that's the way it is in your family.

When an adolescent *manipulates* his parents into changing their decisions, he tends to *lose* respect for his parents. When an adolescent feels that he can *reason with* his parents and thereby sometimes convince them to change their decisions, he tends to *gain* respect for them.

**"After All We've Done for You . . ."**/It's true that parents do a great deal for their children. Of critical importance is: *Why* do they do it? Do parents do things to foster their children's development? Treat them as *human beings* who need guidance, nurturing, and love? Is what they do based upon what their child needs? Or do parents treat their children as *objects* whose purpose is to fulfill parental needs? *Are parents filling the child's needs, or their own?* Are they doing things for their children, not in order to meet the children's needs for nurturing, but to store up credits so that someday they will be paid back? Do they take care of their children so that someday they themselves will be taken care of—or even parented—by their children?

When we do something good or constructive for our children, we should be doing it to help them meet their needs. We should not do things for our children with the expectation that they will someday pay us back or return the favor. That is *using* children, manipulating them to meet parents' needs. Children ultimately will understand this and seldom be grateful for "all you've done for them." Instead of feeling gratitude, they will feel anger and hostility. In all likelihood, *our children will treat us much the same as we treat them.* If we treat our children as separate and worthwhile human beings, they will reciprocate by treating us as separate and worthwhile human beings. If we manipulate our children and treat them as objects—objects whose purpose is to meet our needs and expectations—they will reciprocate by treating us as objects and manipulating us into meeting their needs. The way children get even with their parents is by being like them: a caring person if they have felt cared for; a manipulative person if they have felt manipulated.

If we love our children as individuals and help them meet their own needs without expecting to be paid back, it's not likely that we'll have to throw up our hands and say, "After all we've done for you . . . how *could* you?"

We usually get what we deserve, even from our children.

**"I Don't Have to Have a Reason . . . I'm Your *Parent!*/** Because you *are* his parent, you *must* have a reason. Parents, however, frequently know that their reasons are determined by their own anxieties and fears, are not realistic, and are not based upon the capabilities and characteristics of their adolescent. In such instances, a parent may be tempted to avoid revealing "irrational" reasons by saying, "I don't have to have a reason."

Parents may worry that their adolescent will try drugs, drive too fast, get into trouble, get drunk, become pregnant, etc., and yet realize that it's best not to harp upon these concerns. (Obviously, it would be inadvisable and futile to say, every time your daughter goes out the door, "Now be careful—don't get pregnant, don't get in an accident, and don't try drugs!") What we *can* do is to share with our adolescents that we care about them, are concerned about them, and do worry about them—while, at the same time, leaving their decisions up to them. After all, the decisions do lie with them anyway. A statement of "we trust you to do what you think is right" is often a good way to acknowledge your confidence in your teenager's decisions. In addition, such a statement places the responsibility of behavioral decision-making upon the adolescent—where it belongs. The adolescent is then more likely to make decisions based upon what *he* thinks is right than upon his reaction or response to what *you* want. The decision will then be his, and the process of making up his own mind will have promoted his emotional maturation.

If you share with your adolescent the reasons for your decisions, he will usually reciprocate by sharing his with you. If you don't give reasons for your behavior, you shouldn't expect your adolescent to give reasons for his. One of the best ways to teach our children to be accountable for their behavior is for us to be accountable for ours.

**"You Have No Respect!"**/Adolescents are not noted for unwavering respect for and consideration of their parents—and parents shouldn't *expect* constant respect and consideration. If a teenager based all of his actions upon parental approval, he might never become an adolescent; he would remain a parent-pleasing, parent-dependent child. An adolescent doesn't deliberately attempt to be inconsiderate and disrespectful toward parents; it's just that consideration of parents often takes a temporary back seat to the purposes of adolescence—emotional emancipation and establishment of a separate identity. True respect and consideration of others is an adult stage of moral development and is not a primary goal of adolescent behavior.

The self-centered behavior of adolescents, which does include some inattentiveness to the feelings of parents, is a *temporary* stage. The adolescent is engulfed in "doing his own thing," a "thing" from which parents are excluded. Concentration on oneself is necessary in order to develop one's own identity. As the adolescent becomes more comfortable in his separate self-identity, he will be able to acknowledge, consider, and respect the needs and feelings of others—including those of his parents.

When someone says of a teenager, "My, he acts so grown-up," he is describing either a teenager who has not yet entered adolescence or one who has already completed most of adolescence. They are not describing a typical early or middle adolescent. "He has no respect" may be an appropriate description of a perfectly healthy and normal adolescent.

**"You Don't Understand Anything!"**/It's true that adolescents don't understand many things according to adult logic and adult standards of behavior. If they did, they would be adults, not adolescents. Teenagers view the world primarily through the lens of their own needs, wants, anxieties, and fears. They want to develop their own self-identities, to emancipate from parents, to have a vocation, and to learn how to behave with members of the opposite sex—the tasks of adolescence. Achieving such goals takes years; it takes years to bridge the gap between childhood and adulthood. It's not true that adolescents don't understand *anything* —they just don't understand *everything*. (Who does?) Perhaps one of the great joys of being an adolescent is that one doesn't have the burden of seeing the world through adult eyes.

**"With a Body Like Hers, You'd Think She'd Be More Popular."**/A sexist statement. How often do we hear, "With a body like *his*, you'd think *he'd* be more popular"? In both statements, the adolescent is depicted as a physical object, rather than as a total human being.

A shapely adolescent girl initially tends to have many more problems than rewards. Other adolescents tend to fantasize about her as a "sex object" and relate to her only on a sexual level. Her "body" may scare boys away because of their own normal sexual insecurities. Also, she may become afraid and leery of boys because of their repeated physical advances.

Many people measure "popularity" in terms of numerical success with members of the opposite sex—a narrow and naïve view for adults as much as for adolescents. One of the developmental tasks of adolescence is learning how to get along with and be comfortable with members of the opposite sex—often a slow and painful process. Parents should not be as concerned about the "popularity" of their adolescents as they should be with how well their adolescents are learning to relate to others in a caring and sensitive way.

**"What Did We Raise? An Idiot?"**/Adolescents do the darnedest things—in school, at home, and with their friends—not because they're naïve, uncaring, or unthinking, but because they're adolescents. Not adults, not children. Adolescents.

Neither shackled by adult rationality nor encumbered by childhood innocence, the thinking and behavior typical of adolescents can lead to seemingly incomprehensible stunts. Adolescents don't seem to be as concerned with their behavior as they are with the questions they're attempting to answer through that behavior.

I recall talking to a fifteen-year-old boy who was picked up for taking a car for a "joy ride." He was minimally concerned about the consequences of his actions; he was elated that his friends knew he could drive a car. Another boy almost drowned when he swam across a rapidly moving stream. Nevertheless he was delighted with his feat, because he had proved to his friends (and to himself) that he could do it. Risk-taking behavior does not always represent a wish for self-destruction. It may be an attempt by the adolescent to prove himself powerful, manly, or virile—macho. Although risk-taking behavior may appear "foolish" by adult standards, to the adolescent searching for his self-identity such experimental behavior may represent an attempt to progress through the developmental tasks.

Often the "tenth-grade dip" in school grades reflects the beginning of the adolescent's questioning of parental values and the value of school. "My teachers are dumb," "School's boring, you don't learn anything," and similar attitudes reflect the adolescent developmental process of questioning adult rules and values and the desire to be "independent." Thank goodness, this process in school is often short-lived. Most adolescents soon reapply themselves to learning when its applications to vocational goals and future economic independence become apparent.

No, you didn't raise an idiot. Despite his present behavior, you have probably raised a normal adolescent who will become a competent adult. Meanwhile, some "idiotic" risk-taking and a lot of questioning of parental values are normal components of adolescent behavior.

**"Where Did We Go Wrong?"**/In response to their adolescent's behavior, parents with hands upraised and brows furrowed may ask, "Where did we go wrong?" The fact is, they probably *haven't* gone wrong. If parents measure their adolescent's behavior by adult standards, the behavior might seem to indicate that something is wrong, whereas if parents measure their adolescent's behavior by the purposes and processes of adolescence, the same behavior often can and should be interpreted as healthy and normal.

When *on occasion* our adolescent talks back, breaks a rule, tests out authority, cuts school, tries marijuana, drinks a beer, stays out too late, drives a little too fast, dresses sloppily, etc., we need not feel too distraught. When we place such behavior into perspective, we can see how typical and understandable the behavior may be. We may even derive some joy and satisfaction in seeing our teenagers act like adolescents. We may not like what they do, we may not approve of what they do, we may not understand all they do, but they are doing it—no longer children, not yet adults, but certainly adolescents.

Frequently, only a minor modification in the way we view our adolescent's behavior will permit us to see not where we have gone wrong, but—my goodness!—where we've done something right! We've raised an emotionally healthy—and *typical*—adolescent.

# 11

# "I Think We've Got It Made"

A memorable moment for many parents is when, while discussing their adolescent and appreciating his change into more adultlike behavior, they look fondly and knowingly at one another and say, "I think we've got it made."

The emergence of adultlike behavior is evidenced by gradual, yet distinct, changes in the adolescent's behavior. He is nearing completion of the adolescent growth tasks: establishment of a separate self-identity, emotional emancipation from parents, identification of vocational interests, and development of relationships with members of the opposite sex. Thus he is less dependent upon the behavioral processes (experimentation, alienation, rejection, independent-dependent struggle) he needed to achieve those goals. Signals that the developmental bridge of adolescence is nearly spanned can be seen in the way the adolescent behaves at home, at school, and within the peer group.

## Home

Parents may notice distinct differences in how their adolescent relates to them. He will exhibit less alienating and provoking behavior and seem much less angry at his parents. He begins to discuss issues rather than argue them. He may certainly continue to chide his parents about being old-fashioned, but gone is the angry intensity of his disagreements. Though he may not accept or adopt his parents' opinions and values, he may show respect for them. He may enjoy doing things with his family again; in many ways he "rejoins" the family. He may even visit relatives because he *wants* to, not because he was *told* to do it. In general, he becomes more of a pleasure to have around the house.

These changes in the adolescent's behavior are due primarily to his success in accomplishing the developmental tasks. As the adolescent defines and consolidates his self-identity, and in so doing becomes emotionally emancipated from his parents, he no longer needs to use the behavioral processes that typify adolescent behavior. The more comfortable the adolescent feels in being separate from his parents, the less he needs to act in angry, alienating, and rejecting ways—ways designed to create emotional distance between himself and his parents. Much of the fighting the adolescent has had with his parents was to prove to himself that he could be independent. As he feels more secure in his own abilities and relative independence from his parents, he doesn't feel as threatened by his remaining dependent needs for love, food, clothing, shelter, etc. He realizes that he can retain many dependent needs and still remain relatively independent of his parents. His identity as a separate person is no longer threatened by his remaining dependency upon his parents. More and more he realizes that he is in control of himself and no longer is controlled by his parents. Since he no longer feels controlled, there is much less need to "fight." His newly found confidence in his self-identity, independence, and general abilities helps change the emotionally insecure and often angry adolescent into an emotionally secure and calm young adult. Having broken the shackles of childhood dependency, he can rejoin his family as a young adult.

## School

The adolescent will exhibit a renewed interest in his schoolwork when he sees its relevance to his adult life. He wants to do his homework, cares about school grades, and regards school as an opportunity to prepare for his future vocation. No longer does he view most teachers as incompetent and most courses as irrelevant; he perceives much of the required work as useful and appropriate. Often his classroom behavior improves, and his interests in extracurricular activities at school may be kindled. Overall, he recognizes the value of obtaining an education for both personal and vocational reasons.

## Peers

As the adolescent's self-identity develops and matures, he no longer needs the peer *group* identity; instead, he wants to have his own distinct, *individual* identity. He gives up the group identity and espouses his own ideas and values, rather than relying upon or going along with those of the peer group. Processes used in separating from the peer group are similar to those used previously in separating from parents. Now it's the younger members of the peer group who act stupid, don't understand, and "act so juvenile." Another generation gap occurs, only this time it's between the emerging young adult and his previous peer group.

When he socializes, his groups are distinctly smaller. No longer are forty-three kids crammed into a Volkswagen, nor do hordes of youngsters go out together. Instead, two or three couples get together, and often couples will go out alone. Manners, courtesy, and consideration magically reappear in the way the adolescents treat one another and their parents. Discussions of one's feelings, thoughts, and social issues replace those about cars, clothes, and "teenage idols."

There is less behavioral experimentation, less testing of authority limits, and less experimentation with drugs. Sexual relations tend to be viewed as part of a close emotional relationship rather than as a "What did you get?" experience.

In summary, we can regard the peer group as a "crutch." If you break your leg, you can use a crutch to help you walk while the leg mends. When your leg has healed, you no longer need the crutch, you discard it, and you walk on your own two feet. Similarly, the peer group serves as an "emotional crutch" which helps the adolescent emancipate from his family so that he may begin to establish his self-identity. As his self-identity develops, he no longer needs the "emotional crutch" of the peer group. He leans upon it less and less until, finally, he can discard it and stand alone. He is now an individual with his own separate identity, ideas, and values. An adult.

### Reflection
The end of adolescence is not nearly as turbulent or disruptive a time as its beginning. Certain distinctive behaviors are

hallmarks of the beginning of adolescence; other behaviors mark the emergence of adulthood. When we recognize and understand these typical behaviors, the purposes and processes of adolescence will make more sense.

Adolescents do mature into happy, competent, and worthwhile adults. When you see this happening and say, "I think we've got it made," "all we've done for them" will be worthwhile. You've succeeded as parents. Your adolescent is now an adult.

# Index

Masturbation, 78–79
Middle adolescence, 14–16
Monilial vaginitis, 108–109

Obesity, 53–65
  constitutional, 54–55
  developmental, 55–56
  reactive, 56–60
"One-liners"
  *Adolescent to parent:*
  "All you care about is money!",
    162–163
  "How come the rules are
    different for me?", 169–170
  "I don't care how it was when
    you were my age!", 166–167
  "I hate school!", 165–166
  "Stop treating me like a baby!",
    163–164
  "You can't make me!",
    170–171
  "You don't care about me!",
    167–168
  "You don't understand
    anything!", 165
  *Parent to adolescent:*
  "After all we've done for you
    . . .", 176–177
  "Am I talking to myself?",
    173–174
  "Don't do as I do, do as I say!",
    172–173
  "I can't stand those kids you
    hang around with!",
    174–175
  "I don't care if your friends can
    . . . you can't!", 175–176
  "I don't have to have a
    reason—I'm your parent!",
    177–178
  "We'll see . . .", 171–172
  "What did we raise? An idiot?",
    180–181
  "Where did we go wrong?",
    181–182

"One-liners"—*cont.*
  "With a body like hers, you'd
    think she'd be more
    popular!", 179–180
  "You don't understand
    anything!", 179
  "You have no respect!",
    178–179

Parent-adolescent relationship,
  19–25
Peer group, 10, 14–16
Penis, 82–84
Pregnancy, 84–88
Processes of adolescence, 9, 17
Psychologic developmental tasks,
  8–9
Psychosomatic complaints,
  112–124
Purposes of adolescence, 8–9

Rejection of parents, 9

School, 10, 12–13, 30–31
Self-identity, 8
Sexual behavior, 69–77
  nonsexual motivation for,
    69–73
Sexual experimentation, 73–74
Stages of adolescent behavior,
  9–17
  early adolescence, 10–14
  middle adolescence, 14–16
  late adolescence, 16–17
Suicidal behaviors, 134–139
Syphilis, 103–105

Trichomonas, 105–106

Venereal disease, 99–109
Vocational orientation, 9

Yeast vaginitis, 108–109